101 WAYS TO
MOTIVATE YOURSELF

CHRISTINE INGHAM

KOGAN
PAGE

YOURS TO HAVE AND TO HOLD

BUT NOT TO COPY

First published in 1997

Kogan Page Limited
120 Pentonville Road
London N1 9JN

© Christine Ingham

British Library Cataloguing in Publication Data

A CIP record for this book is available from the British Library.

ISBN 0 7494 2304 8

Typeset by Saxon Graphics Ltd, Derby
Printed in England by Clays Ltd, St Ives plc

Contents

CONTENTS

Working places

Motivation, in brief

When I started telling people I was writing about how to motivate yourself, without fail, everyone's ears pricked up. It was more than polite interest they were showing; they wanted to know the answer: 'I could do with some of that'; 'Quick, tell me how'; 'I'm desperate for some'. Motivation seems to be something almost everyone wants.

Since you too are probably more interested in the 'how to' practicalities (which, incidentally, shows you're already feeling motivated), this overview has been kept brief.

What it is

We all know when we've got it, but appear to have difficulties finding it when we haven't. What is this ephemeral thing?

Motivation is what we feel when we're aroused enough to take action to move towards something we want. What we want can be in the form of a specific reward, or it may be as fleeting as feeling pleased that we've managed to clear our desk of work.

The situation is complicated by the fact that we're not all motivated by the same things. One person will move heaven and earth if they're told their reward will be a week's holiday in the Caribbean, while another remains indifferent – perhaps because they dislike foreign travel. We're all different and we all require different motivators. What we each have to do is find ways in which to make ourselves want, or fool ourselves into wanting, to do whatever needs doing.

What the experts say

There are a range of theories about motivation. Maslow believes that once basic needs are met (like food, warmth, shelter) we then need something higher up the scale to motivate us, like acknowledgement, a sense of achievement, or a sense of belonging. It appears that we like to search out new goals. Once we've got the job to pay for a roof over our heads we look for another challenge to aim for, like promotion within that job. Without having something to strive for, we run the risk of atrophying, of becoming bored, of getting into a rut.

McGregor put forward what was a radical idea at the time: that, given the right conditions, people can actually enjoy their work. Not only that, he also mooted the idea that people like responsibility and to have some degree of control over their work, which is perhaps why self-employment appeals to so many.

McGregor's optimistic view suggests that it is possible for every one of us to enjoy our work; if not wholeheartedly, then at least more than we may be doing at present. In the absence of a model employer, what we need to work on is finding the right conditions ourselves which suit us as individuals.

Another key theory is Herzberg's idea that the things which motivate us are not the same as those which demotivate. According to his findings the sources of demotivation come from the work environment, while those which enthuse us are to be found in the work itself.

Knowing this underlines the importance of finding out not only what motivates but also what demotivates us. There may be many factors, not necessarily all of them to do with the work as such, as Herzberg pointed out. They may be to do with how we feel, how much energy we have, or about having to work in a grotty office, as much as to do with the fact that we may rather be doing something else which motivates us more.

There are many other theories about motivating staff, and in an ideal world we would have line managers who knew about them and put them into practice. But since not many of us have such paragons to work for, what we are concerned with here is how to motivate ourselves.

How to motivate ourselves

Perhaps the best way of all to be highly self-motivated is to work in your dream job. Those who are lucky enough to do so often put up with all manner of what could, for other people, be powerfully demotivating factors: artists living in poverty; animal lovers working in appalling conditions; actors suffering one rejection after another. But if you're doing what you really want to do, these things matter less. You look forward to your job every day regardless; relish each new project which comes along; glide effortlessly through otherwise onerous tasks because you know they're essential to doing the job you like. In this situation motivation doesn't often come into it.

For the rest of us, until our dream jobs happen, we bumble on as best we can and in the meantime try to come to grips with how to raise our levels of motivation when we need to. When we find ourselves up against it we have to find ways in which to remove or overcome the internal barriers which prevent us from tackling the task in hand; to give ourselves a temporary, even illusory, reason for doing it – a carrot by any other name. We can also:

- Change the way the task appears.
- Change the circumstances surrounding it, including the environment (see Way 21, Way 41).
- Change our attitude towards it (see Way 49).
- Alter how we normally tackle it (see Way 55).
- Make changes to ourselves (see Way 7).
- Change the reward (see Way 12).
- Get a new 'stick' (see Way 61).

The strategies we can employ to help us implement these ideas are what form the rest of the book.

Using the book

The suggestions are not in any specific order and are not meant to be read sequentially, unless you particularly want to. Any suggestion might work at any one time, so dipping into the book to find something new to try may be the best way to use it. Perhaps you'll find some which become firm favourites, others which work in one situation but not another, as well as some which may do wonders for a colleague but leave you still with a pile of work undone. Start off with those which have instant appeal because they will already have created within you the right motivational frame of mind to set you off. Try others as the need arises: hopefully you'll discover in the process the key to your own self-motivation, and ways to achieve your own personal goals and ambitions. Good luck.

> 'Find out what you like doing and get someone to pay you for doing it.'
>
> *Katherine Whitehorn*

Way 1 Clear the way – literally

The place where we carry out our job of work tends to stay the same. For the most part it has to. It makes the job easier to have the telephone on one side or the other; current projects stacked on the desk top; writing materials easily to hand. Some people like to keep all this in an orderly, neat and tidy arrangement; others prefer a more 'creative' approach.

However we choose to organise things on our desks, we receive a particular signal when we sit there. The signal is for us to get on with our work; and because we have arranged things in such a way as to help us do that, we slip easily into our usual routine, picking up wherever we may have left off.

At times, though, this normal prompt signal fails. Instead, the scene starts to demotivate us: the piles of work still to do, the same old situation facing us, the reminder of what we have *not* achieved. When we sit down under these circumstances we feel 'bogged down', perhaps falling into a new routine of putting off specific tasks again – even though we know they need doing.

To change the stimulus response, try this: clear away everything off your desk top. Put it on the floor, move it to another desk, or shove it in a cupboard. Just move it all somewhere else, to be retrieved later. Psychologically, this helps in two ways. By engaging in a physical activity we feel as though we are taking action; actually doing something. Also, it produces an illusion of getting lots of work out of the way – instantly. If you're someone who uses the excuse, 'I'll deal with that task when I've got these others out of the way', then this exercise might help. Take no more than ten minutes to clear your work top. Once you've done that, enjoy having acres of space to make a start on the day's work. Without the rest of the normal desk clutter around, you should find focusing on the task in hand that much easier.

Way 2 It only took how long?

We all come across the occasional fly in the workaday ointment; a distasteful task we'd rather ignore. We frown at the

> 'No task is a long one but the task on which one dare not start. It becomes a nightmare.'
>
> *Baudelaire*

thought of it and regularly scowl in its hateful direction. But do it? No.

Favourite excuses for passing over onerous tasks include: 'I'll just finish this other thing first', 'I can't settle down to it right now', 'I need a good clear stretch to get it out of the way', or the ubiquitous, 'I'll do it later'. But no matter how many times these excuses are uttered, the finger of guilt will keep prodding away. Over a cup of coffee you fret at the thought of 'it'. Lying awake in bed your mind turns to the great undone. A scan over your 'To Do' list shows them lingering on – and on.

Adding up the time spent worrying over the task could reveal a figure totalling hours, days – even whole weeks. This is bound to affect your work. It's like trying to run freely towards the horizon while attached to a piece of strong elastic – in this case nailed firmly to that task you're desperately trying to get away from. If you're spending valuable time avoiding a task, rather than letting your motivation plummet even further, try this experiment:

- Make a note of the exact time. Write it down.

- Go and do the task – yes, *that* one.

- Do it in one go – just as an experiment.

- When you've finished, make a note of how long it has taken you.

You may be surprised at how little time it has taken to do what you may have spent hours worrying over: the filing disappears in 30 minutes; the sales appointment is made within five; the difficult letter is dashed off before lunch. And do you feel good about it? You bet.

In future, use this time knowledge. Don't let hours, days or weeks drag by fretting over onerous tasks. Remind yourself how little time it will take to do the chore, after which it will be done, gone, out of the way – freeing you to make real progress with the rest of your work.

Way 3 Back to basics

If you're self-employed you should have, somewhere in the further recesses of the filing cabinet, that all-important document: the business plan. Remember? It's the one you produced to show the world you knew where you were going and how you were going to get there. The document which proudly said, 'I *can* make it – and here's how'.

Although many draw up business plans to help them raise funds, and others to demonstrate to their own satisfaction that a viable market exists somewhere other than in their optimistic hearts, business plans serve another vital function. They are a reminder of your short- and long-term goals, how you are planning to reach them, and in what sort of timeframe. A business plan is a working document. Without one it is easy to lose sight of your aims and, on bad days, wonder what the heck you're doing it all for. That's when motivation feels like it's taken an extended lunch break.

For those who already have a business plan:

DIG IT OUT, DUST IT OFF AND READ IT AGAIN.

It should remind you where you ought to be, and where you are going. Let it rekindle that sense of excitement and anticipation at being on your own personal journey to success. Let it spark your motivation again.

For the rest of us who don't have one, now might be a good time to draw one up. Typically they cover:

- A general statement about the business.
- Your Unique Selling Point (USP).
- The competition.
- Market research – proof that demand and customers exist.
- Marketing – how you drum up business.
- Targets – estimated sales.
- Development plans.
- Your credentials – and how skill shortages are managed.

- The practicalities – location, suppliers, equipment needed, etc.

- A cashflow forecast.

- Accounts for the last three years (if you've been trading that long). Simple graphs can help to highlight existing or developing trends.

By looking objectively at these different elements, areas of difficulty are often highlighted – ones which may well have been adversely affecting your motivation levels.

Once produced, keep this important document to hand and use it regularly. It will help you stay focused, on target – and, even more importantly, motivated.

Way 4 One step at a time

On some grey days, getting on with the work in hand can seem like an almost insurmountable task. We go and make a cup of coffee, have a chat with someone, fill up the day with phone calls which aren't exactly business orientated – anything rather than plough into the pile of work which seems to grow bigger every time we look at it, all of its own accord. Soon it has taken on gargantuan proportions. How on earth can it be tackled? It's enough to make you want to turn tail and run straight for another coffee.

Waiting for the moment to come when there is enough energy and drive to tackle the work all in one go is often futile. Whole days, even weeks, can go by while waiting for that magic moment; for that nano-second when you can say to yourself: 'This is it. I'm ready and I'm going to do it – now!' So, while waiting for that momentous event to happen, you may as well pick up that report you've been putting off and just read through the first paragraph. Only the first one, mind. Let's not get too hasty. It should take one minute, or perhaps two if it's particularly wordy or complex.

Good. You've come through that all right. May as well read another one...

Carry on like this, taking small steps, small bite-sized portions of whatever needs doing. Eventually, the work *will* be completed. Even taking the minutest of steps, the greatest distances can eventually be covered. And what you should find is that, once you've got going, the momentum builds surreptitiously until by the time you next check the clock, you realise you've actually made some progress. At this point, hang on in there, keep going, and take another step – just a small one, mind.

Way 5 Name your problem

There can be any number of reasons why we all at times find ourselves losing our sense of motivation. It is worth spending time considering whether there is a deeper underlying cause, rather than just needing a new carrot – or stick.

One day it may be a work-related issue causing the motivational log-jam; the next, a more personal one. Once whatever is acting as a demotivator is pin-pointed it becomes easier to develop a strategy for tackling it. Unfortunately, the difficulty can lie in identifying the problem in the first place. It is easy to become so embroiled in a problem that we lose track of where it all started.

At school you may have been reprimanded for daydreaming, but here it can help – which is just as well, since it may be what you're doing most of the time anyway. Instead of trying to snap yourself out of it, become more fully aware of those daydreams; capture your thoughts; track down those wanderings. What are they about? Where are they leading? What are they revolving around? Sometimes I startle myself when I do this and realise that what I thought had been wasteful moments were in fact spent working around a work-related or other problem in search of a solution. It may not have been concerned with the task in hand, but it was still productive time. At other times I may be fretting about a certain aspect of the work, or even about something I completed the day before. But until attention is paid to those hamster-wheeling thoughts, a solution is unlikely to be found.

Spend some time trying to identify any specific underlying problems which might be affecting your levels of motivation. Once you've identified them, a solution should easily follow.

Way 6 Building up to down-time

Many people have jobs which produce a more or less steady

flow of work with few peaks and troughs. For others this isn't the case – especially those who are self-employed. Feast or famine seems to be the experience of many who generate their own workloads.

On the plus side, extended breaks between projects can give people time to recharge their batteries, but problems can occur when these down-times take a person's level of motivation plummeting in the same direction. There's a danger that not only your work, but you too, will come to a grinding halt. Trying to start this stationary ball rolling again demands a huge amount of effort and, human nature being what it is, it's more likely you'll decide to wait for the motivation fairy to stop by and pay a visit. It could be a long wait. Better instead to keep things ticking over.

When there is no paying work to do, this is the time to turn to an ongoing stockpile of in-house jobs. This can take the form of a list of those things you always mean to do when you 'have the time'; or it can be a folder or tray containing, for example, non-urgent materials to read through. If you are self-employed, one ongoing task should be to work on developing new ideas and future plans.

Don't forget to include 'treat' tasks as well as more irksome ones on your down-time list – or you may find yourself avoiding it like the plague. And keep it dynamic. Weed out unnecessary items every now and then, and add new ones as they come to you in-between times.

Way 7 Upskilling

Feeling motivated to do a job of work depends partly on whether it presents an appropriate level of challenge. Not enough and we soon start to feel bored. Too much and the work itself begins to act as a demotivator. Finding the right level is crucial if we are to work effectively and stay keen.

If motivation for a project or task is less than 100 per cent, it is worth considering whether the challenge is at that crucial 'appropriate' level – appropriate for *your* skills, that is. It may be you are unsure about how to handle a cold-call to a potential new client; or simply that a look at the new project fills you with dismay. The simple fact may be that you are lacking the necessary skills required to carry out the work. If you have never been taken through how to make cold-calls then it is understandable you will want to avoid making a fool of yourself, or of losing the client you should be winning over. If a new project does not enable you to call on existing skills then you won't feel motivated to tackle it.

Think about the task you feel blocked about. Check whether you have the necessary skills at the appropriate level to do it. If not, motivating yourself to get on and do it will be an arduous, uphill task. Check out how you might fill any skills gaps you do identify. Asking someone already 'in the know' may solve the problem, or signing up for a short course might be in order.

Taking time out to attend professional development courses can often bring additional bonuses. Just being away from the normal place of work and mixing with new people can be a boost in itself. It provides an opportunity to share concerns with like-minded people, renew your interest, glean new ideas and obtain a fresh perspective on your work, which are all helpful in raising overall levels of motivation. But whatever action is needed to update your skills, the sooner it's taken, the better.

> 'Nothing is so fatiguing as the eternal hanging on of an uncompleted task.'
>
> *William James*

Way 8 Imagine when it's done

We all go through those horrid, sticky patches when we just can't seem to make ourselves budge. Hours go by staring at the pile of whatever needs ploughing through but, no matter what, we just can't get going. When inertia of this degree strikes, it is obvious the here and now has turned into somewhere that is a less than enjoyable place to be. Perhaps the future holds the key.

Since you're probably achieving zilch right now other than scoring heavily on the worry meter, take time out for a moment. Let's remove you from the unpleasant present.

Allow your mind to wander for a while and take yourself to a point in time in the near future. This could be no more than half-an-hour away, or it could be a few days hence. The point to aim for is that marvellous moment when the job in hand is finally completed, finished, out of the way. See yourself putting in the last full stop; making the last brush stroke; taking the final page from the printer. Perhaps you can see yourself letting out a deep sigh of relief, stretching, sitting back with the biggest smile ever on your face.

Don't just see yourself – go with the feeling, too. Imagine the sense of accomplishment, the tension easing, the feeling of lightness and sense of relief. Feel the energy flow back into you and through you. Good, huh? You bet. So why deprive yourself any longer of these wonderful sensations? Use the anticipation which the image you conjured up in your mind stimulated. Let it fuel your drive and determination to get on with the work – and start getting it out of the way, now!

Way 9 Is work really the problem?

In some respects it is a shame we are not more like computers, dedicating one file to one issue and another to something else. All neat and tidy – and separate. Unfortunately, our minds don't work like that. Somehow the shopping list file in our brains gets mixed up with the report writing file; the relationship file gets hopelessly entangled with the meeting file. Much as we like to think that when we sit down at our desks we switch exclusively into work mode, that isn't always the case.

Taking the odd moment's mental holiday to think of a loved one is no problem. It provides a micro-break – a bit like coming up for air. But problems can occur when big chunks of time are taken up worrying about issues unrelated to work. When this happens, it not only drains energy – it saps motivation. Let's face it, how can you get excited about doing the accounts when (a) it's not your favourite task anyway, and (b) your mind keeps drifting back to the argument you had last night with your partner/friend/relative?

If you're struggling to generate any enthusiasm for your work, check whether the problem is really to do with leakage from other non-work areas in your life. If it is:

- Take action to deal with the problem if you can (make a phone call; send a card, etc).

- Consciously put worrisome thoughts firmly to one side while you get on with your work – tell yourself you'll deal with them later, or

- Resolve to find professional support if the issues are more serious or ongoing.

Motivation feeds on energy as much as it gives it. If your energy is being leeched away by worries over other concerns, you'll find it difficult to maintain the levels you need to drum up the enthusiasm you want.

Check on whether work really is the problem.

Way 10 Time to expand?

Being self-employed isn't always about wondering where the next customer is going to come from. It is just as common to be inundated with work and almost become a victim of one's own success. Yes, it is wonderful to see customers and clients queuing up for your business, but it can turn sour if the workload becomes too heavy.

With work level issues we're faced with the necessity of finding the optimum level in order to maintain the maximum amount of motivation. We need sufficient work to keep the dynamo humming so that we don't come to a grinding halt, but not so much that we start to burn out.

If you are wondering why, although the business is doing well, you're struggling to find the necessary motivation every day, it may be worth considering whether the workload has passed beyond the critical level for you and has started to become a demotivator. If you find yourself fretting over the growing pile of administrative work, letters to write and filing to sort which you somehow just can't seem to get around to, then it may be time to reassess the level of work you're trying to handle.

There are two ways of managing this situation. One is to expand the business by hiring staff, either to handle time-consuming administrative work or to share the front-line work with; the other is to control the number of clients/customers.

This can be achieved through, for example, increasing the cost of your product/service. This not only automatically eliminates some potential purchasers outside your new price range, but can also increase your profitability: less work for more money. Think about which solution might suit your own situation best.

Way 11 Off-loading

We probably all have some aspects of our jobs about which we feel less than enthusiastic; those items which we try to ignore, knowing full well that the dreadful day will arrive sooner or later when we have to knuckle down and get them out of the way. If they are occasional one-offs which don't take up too much time to deal with, we cope. It is when the drudgery of items which regularly appear on the workaday agenda starts to affect our motivation that something needs to be done.

Just as work is said to fill the time available, thoughts about unpleasant tasks tend to fill each waking moment once they make themselves known. The time we spend fretting and worrying over them can end up draining away every last ounce of motivation for doing anything at all. Each day becomes coloured with the ever-present menace of what we know needs doing – but which we don't want to do. Instead of battling against it, or trying to drum up motivation where none exists, think about whether the task might be off-loaded. For those in employment it might be possible to negotiate a trade-off with a colleague. For those who are self-employed, it is worthwhile considering paying someone else to do it.

If you balk at the thought of more expense, do a scratch calculation of how much of your valuable time it takes not only doing it, but also worrying about the fact you *haven't* done it. And what about the lost productivity, both while you do the task and while you drag yourself around in search of your lost motivation? You'll probably find you'll be much better off hiring someone else to do the work, not only in financial terms but in feeling free to harness the motivation which does exist for the 'real' work you would rather be doing.

Way 12 You're getting there

We can all come unstuck on long-term projects or even on

shorter, less enjoyable ones; when it feels like we'd have more success trying to move a mountain than make the progress we know we should be making.

Authors are particularly prone to this problem. The publisher wants 80,000 words and the deadline's fast approaching, but after slaving all morning there are still another 79,990 to go. An uphill task? Looked at in this way it takes on positively Himalayan proportions.

However, there is another way of looking at things. Instead of focusing on the ground still to be covered, and on today's slow progress, taking a cumulative view is more helpful. It's like looking at the distance covered since leaving the foot of the mountain, rather than since lunch time half-an-hour ago.

Making a graph of this cumulative progress to show the steady progress you're making acts as both a reinforcer (yes, I'm getting there) and as a motivator (look at what I've achieved). What might seem to be an unsatisfactory snail's pace taken on a day-to-day basis is transformed into a helpful indication that you really are getting there.

To draw up a cumulative graph, mark the days of the week (or other time measurement) at equal spaces on the horizontal axis. Mark a measure of your production (in this case, thousands of words) at equal spaces along the vertical axis. At the end of each day, mark on the graph the TOTAL production to date. So, for example, on Monday (day one), I got off to a good start and wrote 4000 words. On Tuesday I did less well and wrote only 3000 – but this still means a total of 7000 words. Wednesday was worse at just 2000 words. Without the graph to show that I was still making *some* progress, I could easily have become demotivated by the end of day three. As it was, I stayed motivated by seeing the word count mount up and Thursday saw a prodigious output of some 4500 words.

No matter how little progress you make, a cumulative graph will register it as a movement in the right direction. Try making one when the going gets tough for you. A quick glance in its direction may be all you need to help spur you on, and on... and on.

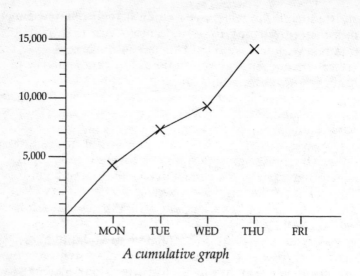

A cumulative graph

Way 13 Beating the clock

We know how vital a stopwatch is to runners in training. It provides an important, objective measurement of their personal performance. Without it they would be in a sort of vacuum, not knowing whether they ran as well as they did yesterday, or had just performed a personal best. The stopwatch provides a measurable and achievable target – key elements in staying motivated.

A stopwatch can also be useful to those of us who are less athletically inclined. For jobs which simply have to be done, regardless of how little we may actually want to do them, a stopwatch can help. It is particularly useful for those jobs which crop up on a regular basis.

Set the stopwatch going and make a start on the task. If legitimate interruptions occur (like an important phone call), stop the clock and restart it again as you resume work. Do the same if the work can't be completed by the end of the day.

Keep the clock running until the task is completely finished. You may be appalled to discover how long it has been dragged out, in which case you may resolve to let it take up only half the time on the next occasion. On the other hand you may be surprised to find it only took relatively few hours (or even minutes). Whichever, make a note of how long it took.

Next time the same job occurs, remind yourself how long it took the last time. Now, see if you can beat it. This strategy won't make you feel any different about the task as such, but it will help to increase your motivation to try and beat your own personal best.

> 'It is impossible to enjoy idling thoroughly unless one has plenty of work to do.'
>
> *Jerome K Jerome*

Way 14 Productivity in perspective

At work, surrounded by equipment of one description or another, it is easy to feel that we too ought to execute our duties at a similarly uniform rate. It hardly needs pointing out that we are not machines, computers or robots. We cannot work tirelessly *ad infinitum*. We just aren't made that way.

Yet despite this, some of us still expect the impossible of ourselves. To give of one's best is one thing, but to push oneself tirelessly can only lead to trouble. At the very least it can lead to demotivation; at worst it may affect one's health.

People who work for themselves may be more prone to falling into this trap. In a normal workplace, colleagues often keep each other in check. They'll drag someone away from their desk to make sure they come up for air every now and then. When people work on their own the lack of interaction can mean a loss of perspective about how hard and intensely they have been working.

It's patently unwise to give in to lapses every time they happen, but if you know you've been working hard it's probably counter-productive to feel guilty about taking an extended lunch break, going for a walk in the park, or treating yourself to an afternoon in front of the television. It can be equally counter-productive to try to work through those times when you know you've had enough for the day. I know it is for me. Make sure you know the difference between feeling a lack of motivation and simply needing to ease your foot off the pedal for a short while.

Remember that we are complex, imperfect beings so be realistic in your expectations of yourself on the work front. Don't feel guilty about slipping down to first gear occasionally. Every now and then it's OK.

Way 15 Strategy meeting

It is difficult for anyone to stay motivated for any length of time without a clear sense of where they are headed. Initially, the thrill of the new is normally enough to keep most people turning up for work every day, but once the novelty has worn off it can start to become a struggle to whip up much enthusiasm if work is taken solely on a day-to-day or task-to-task basis. Eventually, the question arises: 'What's the point?'

For entrepreneur and employed person alike, having a clear idea of where you are going is vital. It provides the 'point'. It justifies to yourself *why* you are doing what you are doing. Even big businesses understand this need, and many have now adopted what they call their mission statement, encompassing their aims and their *raison d'être*. It reminds employers and employees alike what they are collectively striving towards.

For those who are self-employed, knowing where you are heading is crucial and should be something which is addressed in your business plan (see Way 3). Without having it clearly identified it is all too easy to find oneself adrift, bogged down by the mundane, having forgotten the hopes and aspirations which fired your enthusiasm when you first started.

Employees also need to have their sights set. Justification for doing the work may be linked into an overall career plan; a desire to make a contribution in a particular field; or because it enables them to fulfil other aims outside work.

Whether you are working for yourself or someone else, having a clear idea of where you are heading will help to give that vital boost on those grey days when your motivation seems to desert you. Think about where you are heading, how you are going to get there, and clarify in your own mind the justification for doing what you are doing – your own personal mission statement.

Way 16 Brainstorming for beginners

Brainstorming is a well-known business technique used to help solve problems. It involves groups of people coming together and suggesting possible solutions to problems 'off the top of their heads'. Ideas are uncensored. In a brainstorming session, any suggestion is acceptable. All are noted down by the group's facilitator. Debate or comments about the relative merit or workability of each are withheld until the brainstorming has finished. The aim is to generate as many ideas as possible, no matter how wacky or impractical they might appear.

This same technique can be used when you feel you've come to a dead end, motivationally speaking, with a project or aspect of work. Brainstorming can help you find unusual solutions when the work needs to be done but the prospect of doing it palls. A fresh approach may be all that's needed.

Find a willing friend or colleague to help. Explain the problem and tell them how to brainstorm if they don't already know. Note down every idea, comment, suggestion or solution as it comes. Remember not to pass judgement at this stage or even make any remarks about offerings. The flow of ideas can easily be blocked by uttering the wrong word. A brainstorming session need only last for between 15 and 30 minutes, or as long as the ideas keep coming. When you have finished, a more careful look can be taken at the list you have generated. Hopefully, there will be at least one idea which can bring that fresh approach you have been looking for and which will give a boost to those flagging levels of motivation.

Way 17 The smell of success

Every now and then we all need some sort of boost to help us make it through the next stage of a job. Breaking off for a few minutes is normally enough when work is going well, but on those days when we find ourselves struggling to make the effort it may not be enough.

Since our sense of smell acts almost immediately on the brain, using aromatherapy oils may provide the lift you need. For hundreds of years people have benefited from the restorative effects of essential oils. Not only can they help alleviate physical symptoms, they are also beneficial in treating mental and emotional states.

There are a number which may be worth investigating when your enthusiasm is on the wane:

- Basil: is uplifting, refreshing and brings clarity to the mind.
- Bergamot: uplifting when you're feeling low.
- Clary sage: lifts the spirits too, but also relaxes and brings on a sense of well-being.
- Grapefruit: said to encourage positive feelings.
- Rosemary: helps clear thoughts and sharpen the mind.
- Ylang ylang: lifts the spirits and brings on a sense of euphoria.

Oils can be used singly, or combined to bring about complementary effects. For example, you might choose to try basil and rosemary together.

Buy pure essential oils rather than diluted ones. Use them in a diffuser which can be picked up cheaply from health stores and some high street chemists. Alternatively, place a small damp towel on a radiator and put one or two drops of your chosen oil(s) on it. As the aroma fills the room you should, according to the aromatherapists, soon notice a change in your state of mind – and hopefully find you're once again raring to go.

Way 18 Workaholism doesn't work

We all put in the extra time on occasions, but workaholics put it in all the time. You know you're in trouble if you can't switch off from work, or feel uncomfortable, even anxious, if you do. If you're eating, breathing and sleeping work, and starting to wonder where your motivation has gone, you may be overworking.

Fear is what drives people into workaholism: fear of failure; fear of loss of control; fear of there being nothing else if time isn't filled with work. 'But I love the high I get from it,' you might say. What's probably happened is that you have become addicted to the adrenalin rush it gives. It's still, however, an addiction – and any addiction is unhealthy.

Besides it eventually starting to demotivate, overworking can also lead to stress, relationship difficulties, lower productivity (paradoxically), irritability and health problems, to name but a few. This may not be evident over the short term, but will become so the longer it continues.

People with addictions are, typically, not in touch enough with their own personal reality to be able to recognise when problems are starting to occur. Denial is the more likely reaction. So before things progress too far down that particular route, take a few moments out for reflection. Make an honest appraisal of how many hours you currently spend working, thinking or worrying about work. Consider the overall balance of your lifestyle. Do you socialise regularly? Do you spend enough time with friends and loved ones? Do you have ways in which you can indulge yourself on a regular basis?

A few simple adjustments to your lifestyle should bring back a sense of balance to your life and help you feel renewed and energised again, but do stay alert to the problem. Working hard is one thing but if your motivation takes a nose-dive, check out whether you've unwittingly over-stepped the boundary again and strayed into the realms of overwork.

Way 19 Start of the day routine

Exercising the self-discipline needed to get oneself off the starting block in the morning can turn into a stumbling block instead for many of us – one which can last throughout the day if we're not careful, especially when working at home. There are just so many temptations: the washing up, making a slice of toast, doing a bit of tidying up, reading the newspaper, to say nothing of the dreaded daytime television. But for anyone, employed or self-employed, at home or in the office, how the morning starts can make or mar the rest of the day.

The problem for some people can be with not being able to 'get it together'. Until the brain's in gear, too much time is spent pottering around and letting oneself be distracted. Constructive thinking and planning (let alone doing) seems beyond them. If this is your problem, try solving it by working out a prearranged routine; one which helps you become productive as soon as your behind touches the swivel chair. A routine which you can slip into easily without having to *think* about it, for example filing for 15 minutes, updating records for half an hour or you might even arrange to have regular team meetings to start the day.

You may decide to have a different routine for each day of the week, or you could decide to have the same one each day. Choose whatever works best for you.

If you're self-employed it may also help to establish a routine which provides a clearer psychological cut-off from the domestic scene than just shuffling off into the back room. Going out for a newspaper is one way, making sure you head straight to your work space on your return and not for the comfy chair in the lounge.

Once your routine becomes established it should help overcome the slow-start syndrome which besets many of us, putting you in the right frame of mind to achieve for the rest of the day.

Way 20 Stalemate?

Having stability in a job has obvious benefits. It allows a person to build up their confidence and expertise, while on the personal level it makes it easier to enjoy their non-working lives. Difficulties can arise when the job presents few challenges any more. Without enough challenges there may be little to motivate, and work may soon become a drag.

Although the answer for some might be to look for another job, for others this may not be possible, necessary or even desirable. There may be too many other plus points to staying put: good work colleagues, convenient location, good in-work benefits. For someone who is self-employed, looking elsewhere for work may be even less appropriate a suggestion.

A more useful option is to find ways to introduce the type of challenge which may be missing at present into your existing job, and provide the sort of positive stimulus to fire your enthusiasm once more. Depending on your situation, think about how you might do this. You might sign up for a training course; meet with supervisors to discuss changes to your job description; put your name forward to sit on groups or committees; discuss paths to promotion with bosses.

If you're self-employed there may be an even greater range of options open. Now might be the time to look into exporting; relocating to sunnier climes; finding out about awards your business might win; moving into a different market; targeting different clients.

Spend some time thinking about which challenges would infuse you with a new sense of direction and the sort of energy and drive you may feel is presently missing from your humdrum working life.

Way 21 Lighting the way

Lighting may not necessarily be seen as a particularly important consideration in the workplace, except in retail environments where it is put to good effect for the benefit of buying customers. Yet lighting can affect a person's work, efficiency and even stress levels. Poor lighting may be subtly affecting your overall enthusiasm for sitting down and getting on with the job of work without you even realising it.

- Make sure computer screens have no direct light shining on them. Glare strains the eyes, slows down work and increases the chance of making mistakes. Ambient lighting works best. Angle lights upwards to bounce off ceilings.

- Make sure spotlights are not shining into your eyes or creating shadows over your work.

- Adjustable desk lamps allow light to be directed where it is needed.

- Try using daylight simulation bulbs which provide a more natural lighting effect.

Also, make sure you are getting enough natural daylight throughout the day. Some people have found they are particularly badly affected by lack of light during the winter months and experience bouts of depression known as Seasonal Affective Disorder as a result. Special full-spectrum light-boxes can be used to help top-up their daylight requirements. Overhead lighting strips are also available.

It is worth checking out the lighting at your place of work and making any necessary adjustments. Improved lighting won't make you feel more motivated about a job which you essentially loathe, but it can help to create a more appealing work environment and deal with the subtle difficulties which poor lighting can create.

Spectra Lighting, York House, Lower Harlestone, Northampton NN7 4EW; 01604 821904.

Way 22 Relocate

Facing the same work surroundings every day means they are hardly likely to offer inspiration, especially when trying to get yourself to sit down and tackle a particularly unwelcome task. On occasion I've found that relocating to a new, temporary environment helps to nudge me out of my inertia and start to tackle whatever I've had difficulty getting down to – like the accounts last week.

Any new location which you find pleasant will do to provide the additional stimulus. In the past I've temporarily relocated to the reference library, a friend's flat, the park and a café. I've still to try a museum, the beach, an art gallery, the car and the rather smart office of a friend of mine.

If you're employed, try negotiating with your boss to work at home for the day – or in another location. If they are concerned about not being able to contact you, offer to phone in every hour. Less drastically, try changing desks with someone else in the same office for the afternoon while you make a start on the report you've been avoiding. Or change your desk around so that it faces another way.

If you're self-employed, think about whether your place of work is helping or hindering you. It may be that you've outgrown your present premises and need to consider a more permanent relocation. If you work at home, perhaps the time has come to rent an office space .

When self-motivation is sagging, putting yourself in a different environment can help to create a new, albeit temporary, set of circumstances; a new framework in which to work – it may be just what you need to get you going again.

Way 23 Routine or not routine

We need routines in our lives to make them workable. Without some sort of structure to the working day and week it is easy to slip into inefficient and unproductive ways. There is a risk, though. Our daily routines can start to stifle us, fail to foster interest in what we're doing, and even send us into an almost automaton-like trance. Hardly the right circumstances in which to nudge our motivation into a state of readiness and alert. We're more likely to slip into a stupor.

So, although having a workable routine is important, think about how long it has been since you last varied it. Breaking the pattern of how we do things adds spontaneity and in its turn enlivens, so if you suspect you have been treading the same old path for too long, try taking a departure from it.

Depending on how much flexibility you have available to you, consider:

- Changing the hours you work – eg have a four-hour break at midday and work longer in the evening.

- Swap afternoon duties with morning ones.

- Think of other ways of changing the running order of your day.

- If you normally chair meetings, ask someone else to run the next one.

- Ask others how they perform a task and try their way for a change.

- Plan alternative lunch time venues or activities.

Think of other ways you might make some alterations, either permanently or just for a day.

Routines can stultify, which is why holidays are so important – and so beneficial. Instead of waiting for the next one, give yourself a mini-break and see how much you benefit from a simple change in routine.

Way 24 Role models

Everybody has their own particular strengths – and weaknesses. What one person finds a breeze, someone else struggles with for days. Jenny admires the way you can plan meetings; but you would love to have her way with budgeting. If only we could all swap skills occaisionally, we'd be able to solve the problem of having to deal with tasks we'd rather avoid.

The next best thing to becoming another person, complete with all the talents you need and admire, is to try to emulate them. Having identified Jenny as someone who is good with finance, make use of the good example she sets. Instead of envying her skills, use her as a role model. It doesn't matter whether you personally know your chosen role model. You might simply work in the same company as them, or just know them by reputation. The important thing is to identify someone who acts in the way you would like to, or has achieved what you aspire to.

Using someone as a role model doesn't mean aping them like a juvenile pop fan. What it does mean is making positive and practical use of what you see as examples of good practice. This may mean approaching and handling tasks in the same way as another person. Or it may mean simply adopting the same attitude – some people act more confidently than others, or have a 'can do' attitude which helps them win through. If these are the qualities you think you would find useful in tackling a particularly onerous task, try to put yourself in the same frame of mind as this other person; adopt the same mental stance. You might also consider asking them for more direct input: how does Jenny go about estimating her outgoings so accurately? Perhaps she uses a different method from your 'guesstimate' approach.

As children we learn from the way we see people acting around us. Learning from example is as valid for us as adults in the work environment as it is for children in the playpen. A good role model can offer a useful guide to striking the right attitude for handling situations or tasks about which you may otherwise feel less than inspired.

Way 25 Programme yourself to work

Neuro-Linguistic Programming (NLP) sounds complex but is simply a method of enabling people to 'reprogramme' themselves in order to replace unhelpful behaviour patterns with more useful ones. Anthony Robbins in his book *Unlimited Power* defines NLP as 'the study of how language, both verbal and non-verbal, affects our nervous system... In short, it is the science of how to run your brain in an optimal way to produce the results you desire'.

The way NLP works is based on learning to identify what triggers your behaviour and whether you are a visually-, auditorially- or kinesthetically (touch)-orientated person. For example, a visually-orientated person will use lots of visual language: 'I see the problem,' 'It looks to me like...'. Using this knowledge, reprogramming involves learning techniques, skills and interventions which produce rapid changes in behaviour.

NLP is successfully used in management training to help individuals achieve more. It is an empowering method; a tool for change which enables people to realise their potential to transform actions – or even take action in the first place. The techniques show how to redirect mental activity and switch into a more helpful, positive mental state.

If you like the sound of a method which can help to change your way of thinking and approach to work, further details can be obtained from:

Association for Neuro-Linguistic Programming, 100B Carysfort Road, London N16 9AP; 0171 241 3664.

Way 26 Exercise – macro

With all the publicity over recent years about the benefits of exercise, we all ought to be out there every day doing our physical best to perk ourselves up. Unfortunately we're not – well, not all of us. Yet the benefits are spelt out for us: increased health benefits reduced risk of illness; more energy; and what perhaps concerns us most here – an enhanced sense of well-being.

Having a desk-bound or other sedentary job means our bodies are inevitably going to become sluggish. Circulation slows down, breathing becomes more shallow, muscles lose tone; hardly a recipe for feeling alive, vibrant and mentally alert. Exercise is important, not just for our bodies but also for how we feel mentally. If your brain feels fuzzy around the edges and you're having difficulty raising enthusiasm for what you're doing, exercise may provide at least part of a solution.

Joining the body-builders down at the gym is not for everyone. An activity which can more easily be integrated into the day and suit the demands of your lifestyle is more likely to succeed. Walking is as good an aerobic activity as jumping around in a leotard. Think of how it might be included in your day's activities: walk briskly to and/or from the next bus stop; use a more distant shop or cafe at lunch time; offer to walk a neighbour's dog; use the stairs instead of the lift; or run up the ones you already use.

There are lots of videos and books available for those who prefer to do exercise routines in the comfort and privacy of their own home. You might even hire a personal trainer to come and put you through your paces. Also, think about learning a new sport or form of exercise, like T'ai Chi or yoga. Exercise can relax as well as enliven. Feeling motivated requires energy and it comes more easily when you're feeling good. If exercise is lacking from your life, putting it back in may help you put more effort back into your work.

> 'Energy is the power that drives every human being. It is not lost by exertion but maintained by it.'
>
> *Germaine Greer*

Way 27 Exercise – micro

In Way 26 we looked at the importance of exercise in helping to liven ourselves up and provide an enhanced sense of well-being. When we're stuck inside all day we might also benefit from an additional boost to sharpen the dulled edge, perk up the system and help us get down to whatever needs doing.

Excusing yourself for a quick jog around the block may not be possible – but micro-exercising might. This refers to movements which stimulate the circulation and stop muscles from becoming cramped. It can be as simple as taking a good, long stretch while still sitting down. Even this can be enough to send fresh oxygen to the muscles and get the circulation moving again. It only takes a few seconds but can help to refresh you when you're starting to switch off from your work – especially when working on a lengthy task. Try to make sure you have a stretch at regular intervals, say every 40 minutes or so.

Still sitting, you can also lean over to one side and then the other to stretch the rib cage. Bend forwards to flex the spine. If you have the time, stand up and flex backwards too, supporting your back by putting your hands on your hips. Don't forget to stretch the legs out as well. As you move around, take in a couple of deep breaths, too. Again, it will get the circulation going, bringing more oxygen to the brain which will help you feel refreshed.

If you're feeling sluggish you're unlikely to be inclined to put much energy into work. Taking micro-exercise breaks can help to prevent you from slipping into lethargy and provide the boost you need to stop you from becoming stale.

Way 28 Up the ante

When there's an unpleasant task to be done it can seem to take forever: first to get around to making a start, and secondly to get it eventually out of the way. Like a bad smell, these tasks tend to linger on.

We all know it's not unusual for tasks like these to end up being done in a frantic rush, just before the deadline is due. It matters not that you may have had the last month in which to complete it all. Come the final Friday of the last week and there you are, working like mad to finish on time. The problem is rarely to do with the level of difficulty, nor the timescale. Yet it is only when the chips are down and the pressure is on that the work gets done. Somehow when the task or circumstances surrounding it become more difficult, we become more motivated to do it.

This strange motivational quirk can be turned to our advantage. If you're struggling to make a start on something, try upping the ante: make it more difficult for yourself, more challenging. If you have five cold calls to make, give yourself more to do; if you have until the end of next week to hand a project in, bring the deadline forward and only give yourself until the end of today instead; if you have to have a speech ready by the end of the week, imagine the conference has been brought forward to tomorrow.

When a task in itself fails to motivate sufficiently, think about how you might make it more challenging. Setting a new deadline, increasing the target or turning it into a more complex operation then becomes the new focus of motivation. Put the pressure on and, paradoxically, you may find yourself *more* motivated than before to knuckle down.

Way 29 Naps, siestas and 40 winks

If you feel tired it is unlikely that your motivation levels will be at their peak, so without further ado make sure you are getting enough good quality sleep at night. However, even if you are, you might benefit from allowing your body to recharge its batteries during the day by taking a quick 40 winks.

Many people feel their energy levels drop off after lunch. Lecturers and teachers are only too aware of this problem. This is the time when audiences are more likely to find concentration difficult and to switch off – or even doze off. If this is a problem you have, try finding a quiet place after eating lunch, and close your eyes for 10 or 15 minutes. Set an alarm or arrange for someone to check on you if you're worried about the nap turning into an hour-long snore.

Although naps can be most helpful, it is not necessary to actually go to sleep in order to feel refreshed. Dr Herbert Benson at Harvard University studied the beneficial effects of deep relaxation achieved through meditation and other practices. Learning how to switch into this mode involves relaxing the body and quietening the mind without falling asleep, and can leave a person feeling as refreshed and invigorated as if they had dozed off completely.

If you suspect one of the reasons for your lack of motivation is that you're just plain dog tired, try integrating a quiet nap into your day. Recharging your batteries may provide the extra energy you need to get the job done.

Way 30 Work expands

Parkinson's Law says that work expands to fill the time available. If there are three small tasks to complete in a working week it is more than likely it will take all five days to grind slowly through them. Should the pace increase dramatically and four more tasks sneak on to the list, all needing to be completed a day earlier, they too will somehow be finished in time.

In Way 28, we looked at how making tasks more challenging can act as a motivator. Similarly, one of the best ways of motivating yourself to clear a backlog of jobs is to take on more work, so that in essence the task which has been plaguing you becomes just one of many. Instead of giving it all the time it needs in which to expand and seemingly grow in size and menace, restrict it. Haul in the boundaries. Crop it back. Squeeze it into a tiny little space, cramped in between other more important, enjoyable, easier tasks. Don't let it bully you. Show it who's boss. Put it in its place and watch it become more manageable, even insignificant.

When it has been reduced to less intimidating proportions, and with the pressure of other tasks needing to be done as well, you should find it much easier to deal with it summarily; to clear it out of the way, almost before you realise it. Of course, there's still the rest of the work to deal with!

Way 31 Work = money

Remember the thrill of your first pay packet, or the first time a client paid you? Unfortunately, over time we lose that sense of excitement and start to take it all for granted. We tend to forget that money is being paid over to us in exchange for making our time and skills available to others.

Money can be one of the best motivators, but it does lose its impact once we start to overlook the importance of this exchange. After all, it's just a salary, we think; another cheque to cover the bills; a meaningless transaction between two remote bank accounts. No wonder it fails to motivate if we look at it in this way.

Take a fresh look at your earnings and see if it can rekindle that power to motivate. Once, when employed and struggling to make it through a particularly unwelcome task, I did exactly this. I was on a salary and realised I had no idea how much my time was worth, so I sat down and worked out how much I was being paid by the hour – then by the minute. It was enlightening, to say the least. Bringing my yearly income down to a more meaningful level of how much I had earned in the last five, ten, 15 minutes, I was suddenly reminded of the link between what I was doing and the reward I received. It worked. Looking at the horrid task again, I appreciated more fully that completing it would earn me an hour's pay, if not more. It suddenly seemed like I was earning 'real' money. By five o'clock I'd earned myself a new pair of jeans! Think about the other benefits of receiving money for what you do: the home you're able to live in; the holidays you take; the leisure time you're able to enjoy.

If you're self-employed, the link between work and money is even more acute. No work equals no pay. When the bank balance is flush, it may not seem so important; so a quick recall of more difficult times in the past, or of what you are aiming towards in the future can help.

As we all know, money isn't everything, but reminding ourselves not to take it for granted can be a great motivator at times. *Spend* a minute or two reflecting on your worth and the link between what you do and the money you earn. And if you're not satisfied with the exchange, perhaps now is the time to ask for a raise, increase your prices – or find a better-paid job.

Way 32 Forward planning

The tasks we don't want to do are often those we are able to procrastinate over without it causing too much of an immediate problem. Except it does. We waste valuable time and energy. Yet somehow, even as the pressure mounts, we still find it almost impossible to get on with it.

A helpful strategy is to sit down, not to do the work as such, but to plan out how and when it is to be done. Take out your desk diary or personal organiser. Have another look at the task or project you've been avoiding. If it is work in general you're having difficulty with rather than a specific item, pull together a list of outstanding work. Assess what needs doing with each task, breaking them down into more manageable parts.

When you've done this, use your diary to book in times over the following days or weeks to work on each project. For example, you could start making in-roads into doing your accounts by booking yourself some time this afternoon in which to organise the receipts and put them in order. When it's completed, put the task away. If that's what you planned to do, that's all the work you need do on it today.

When you turn up for work the next day, your diary tells you the second half of the morning is to be spent totalling the receipts you put in order the day before. Again, when completed, put the work away and in the afternoon proceed with whatever other task has been booked in. Continue like this until the work is completed – or you're on such a roll you don't need the plan any more.

However, since we live in the real world there is every likelihood the plan will go awry. When this happens, don't beat yourself up about it – simply make the necessary readjustments and start afresh with the revised plan the following day.

Planning out the work and actually writing it down in a diary helps by making it appear that someone else is giving us instructions to follow when we open the page and see a specific task written down. It absolves us of the responsibility for deciding whether or not to make today the day we make a start on the dreaded project. The decision is made for us (albeit by ourselves) to actually do something. If you're making little headway with your work, try this strategy. Even the act of drawing up a timetable can sometimes be enough to break the log jam and get things moving again.

Way 33 All stand

We turn up for work and tend to do the same old thing. We even sit in the same position, often for hours on end, our bodies becoming more lethargic the longer we sit there brooding over our work. Allowing our bodies to remain static for long periods means we become sluggish – and can eventually find it difficult to think at anything faster than a snail's pace.

We've already looked at how exercise can help in Way 26 and Way 27. Feeling more energetic means you're more likely to feel capable of rallying round, lifting yourself out of your torpor and applying yourself to work. Besides exercising, another idea which some people find useful is to alternate between sitting and standing. This isn't an excuse to lounge around while the work lies waiting back at the desk or workstation. It means working while standing up at intervals throughout the day.

See if you can find or arrange an elbow-height work surface to use. It should be high enough that you don't have to bend to use it. Also, try to make an effort to stand at other times too, for example when using the telephone, having a talk with someone or arranging papers. Alternatively, if you spend most of your time standing, use a high stool to sit on at intervals to give your body a rest from its regular stance.

Changing positions wakes our bodies up and helps renew energy, as well as providing a novel and stimulating change. If you spend most of your time in one position, try adopting a new one to see how it affects you.

Way 34 Self-hypnosis

One way or another most of us eventually manage to break through our blocks about work. With a little push we start the ball rolling, perhaps after putting into practice one or two of the suggestions in this book. But unfortunately for some, work avoidance can become so deep-seated it turns into an almost habitual response. And we all know how difficult habits are to break.

In cases like these, many people have found hypnosis and self-hypnosis helpful. It enables them to break through the negative, unhelpful patterns which are holding them back, and replace them with positive, enabling ones which help them move forward. If your work avoidance has become chronic and other tactics fail, learning how to hypnotise yourself might do the trick. Hypnotism is also useful even if you have no problems as such but would simply like to improve your productivity, creativity or rate of success.

Despite its dubious past reputation, hypnosis is now an acceptable complementary therapy. It works by accessing the subconscious, where all our nasty habits lie lurking. A state of deep relaxation of both body and mind is created by listening to a carefully worded script. Once this state has been reached, a positive suggestion regarding the desired change in behaviour is made. Sessions are brought to an end by your being counted back to full consciousness.

If you think this might be the answer to your motivation problems a do-it-yourself approach is possible by listening to a recording of either your own voice reading a pre-planned script or that of a therapist. To find out how, read *Self Hypnosis* by Valerie Austin or any of the other books available on this subject.

Way 35 I've started, so...

We all know the longer we put off a task, the worse it seems. As another day passes leaving the work still undone, it starts to seem as if only gargantuan-sized efforts on our part will be enough to see it through. Part of the problem lies in the time we waste pondering how on earth we are to summon the superhuman reserves the job seems to warrant. No wonder we feel a sense of defeat every time we think about it.

Instead of focusing on the gigantic task as a whole, try concentrating on making just the tiniest step forward to create a more accessible in-road into it. For example, let's say I'm stuck on a particular chapter of a new book. After all the normal anxious outpourings about ever being able to write it at all, I take a new tack and resolve to forget about the chapter in its entirety, focusing instead on just the first paragraph. If I'm having a really bad time I deal with just the first sentence.

When I do this it takes the pressure off me to write the chapter's full 4000 words, the anxiety drops away and, as if by magic, my mind starts to feel free again. In this happier frame of mind, and knowing I have only to concentrate on a few sentences at most, this more manageable task is soon completed. And with one paragraph done the first sentence to the next one starts to form. And before I realise it, I'm tapping away making good headway on the chapter I thought would never see completion.

See if you too can find a way of making even the smallest start on whatever you're avoiding. Once you've started, you may find it easier than you thought to stick at it until that blissful moment when the whole thing is at last finished.

Way 36 What's your trigger?

Trying to find the solution to a lack of self-motivation can be nothing short of exasperating. We all know when we've got it, but never know how to find it when we haven't. It's worse than trying to solve an Agatha Christie mystery.

What motivates each of us can vary enormously from person to person. What acts as a potent trigger for one may leave another wondering what all the excitement is about. 'It helped me clear my desk in no time,' they shout excitedly, but it falls on deaf ears with others for whom the spark fails to ignite. We are all individual; and our motivation requirements are very different.

This may provide us with a clue. Next time you're fired up and raring to go, pause for a second or two to consider why today is different. What is it about the work which appeals? Have any changes occurred within you? Why is it so much easier to make a start on it than something else you've been struggling with? What are the circumstances surrounding it which may have a direct or indirect bearing on it? Consider the nature of the task and your motivation for it from as many different angles as you can. Draw on this information next time you hit a bad patch. Are there any conditions you could duplicate for this new task? Could you approach it in the same way as you did the other? What changes to the circumstances surrounding it could you make so that it more closely resembles the other?

By starting to understand our own personal triggers we can more easily adopt particular strategies and introduce those sets of circumstances which help us find our own Holy Grail of self-motivation. Shakespeare wrote, 'The fault... is not in our stars, but in ourselves' – which is where we too might find the key to what motivates us.

Way 37 Endings and beginnings

Trying to make a productive start to an unplanned day is like sitting down to eat but finding nothing ready on the table. It's frustrating, demotivating and makes for a difficult start – hardly the best or easiest way to begin. Getting off to a good start (or bad) can set the tone for the rest of the day.

It can be an awkward hurdle to overcome but the answer may lie in a little pre-planning. You could attempt to do this first thing in the morning, but that assumes you'll feel up to it. What happens if you don't? We all know the answer to this, from experience. We start pottering around; busying ourselves with unimportant bits and pieces; putting off the more pressing work we know we should be doing.

A better way is to spend a few minutes *at the end of the day* to map out the following day's itinerary. This can be easily integrated into the winding down process, when you start to clear away the day's debris off the desk, put projects to one side and collect files together. While doing this you'll probably find yourself reviewing in your mind the progress you've made and will automatically be reminded of things you had meant to do or which still need to be done. This provides the starting point and raw material for drawing up the following day's plan. Jot down what comes to mind, add any other items which need doing, put it in some sort of order, and put the list in your diary or somewhere else you'll see it first thing. Come the next morning, the hard thinking part has already been done. Before your procrastinating self can get a foot in the door you're already off the starting block, making the first phone call on your ready-prepared list.

Start to use the down-time at the end of one day to plan out the next. It can bring a sense of control and order, and make it easier to kick-start yourself to begin each day on a more successful note.

Way 38 Energy foods

Building levels of motivation requires a fair amount of energy. Without it, slumping in our chairs seems far preferable to moving ourselves forward – and at times it is all we're capable of. In order for our bodies to generate the energy we need, we must provide it with the right sort of fuel – that is, we must eat properly.

Nutritionists suggest that eating foods which provide a slow, consistent release of energy is more helpful. Try high-protein foods like fish and meat (if you eat these), cheese, nuts and eggs; or, if you're vegetarian, protein combinations like bean-based dishes with rices or wholemeal breads – beans-on toast is ideal. Fresh cooked or raw vegetables are also good energy foods. What doesn't help is eating processed or refined foods like pies, pasties and white bread sandwiches or rolls.

If you tend to feel lethargic after eating at lunch time, consider food combining. This means eating only certain types of food together and avoiding those combinations which may deplete energy and lead to tiredness while they are being digested. Apparently it's fine to eat proteins (eg meat, fish, eggs) and highly acid fruits (eg oranges, apples, gooseberries) in the same meal, but carbohydrates (eg bread, potatoes, rice, pastries) should be eaten at another time. Green vegetables combine well with any food. So an omelette and salad, or vegetable curry, followed by an orange would be great; a ham and cheese sandwich with a slice of apple pie wouldn't.

Throughout the working day maintain good energy levels by grazing on healthy nibbles. Nuts, seeds and crudités are all excellent. Be careful with fruit, especially dried fruit, with its high natural sugar content. They too can lead to tiredness. (Bananas positively send me to sleep!)

Start to play around with the type of foods you eat. Experiment a little. Find out which foods maintain your energy throughout the day and which deplete your energy levels. With a few careful adjustments to your daily food intake you could find you have more than enough energy to summon the motivation you need.

Way 39 Using a timer

A few years ago when I was recovering from a painful slipped disc, part of the therapy involved moving from my normal sitting position at the computer every 20 minutes or so to flex my back. The only problem was that more often than not I would be so immersed in my work that I'd completely forget about it until much later.

It was when I was walking around a kitchenware shop that I found the answer in the shape of a small kitchen timer; the sort with a dial which counts down from anything up to 60 minutes. With this I could set it to ring for the short time periods I needed and it proved to be much more efficient at remembering than I was. However, I soon found another use for it, too – in helping me make progress on projects I had been finding it difficult to make a start on.

I would set the timer to, say, 15 minutes or half-an-hour, choosing a time period I felt comfortable with; one which matched the amount of motivation I felt I could summon. This meant I was setting a realistic limit for myself. As a result I felt reasonably happy, knowing I only had to get my head down for just the 15 or 30 minutes. The prompt from the timer reminded me to stop working before I started to feel bored, tired or demotivated again. More often than not I was pleasantly surprised when the bell rang telling me to finish. I frequently didn't realise I'd been working for as long as I had, which meant each session ended on a high. Eventually, after a few more timer-controlled sessions, the work was soon completed.

Now, I wouldn't be without my kitchen timer. They're not expensive to buy (you may even have one already), so try putting one to use to see if it can help you make progress with your work instead of waiting for the motivation fairy to pay you a long overdue visit.

Way 40 Some like it hot

Anything which causes discomfort is a distraction from work and provides too easy a justification for not tackling what needs doing. If it's extreme enough the level of discomfort can lead to stress, sapping that vital energy required to keep your motivation at its peak.

A surefire way to feel uncomfortable is by having room temperatures set at an inappropriate level. Too hot and we become lethargic and unable to concentrate, especially if the air is stuffy and stale as well. Too cold and our muscles contract, making us feel tense and unable to relax well enough to concentrate effectively on our work. The statutory required minimum temperature is 16 degrees Celsius.

If the temperature dial is set either too high or low to suit your own personal preferences:

- Wear outfits with multiple layers which can easily be adjusted to suit how hot or cold you feel.
- Check for draughts.
- If it's just your extremities which suffer, wear ankle boots, tights or thicker socks.
- Investigate the possibility of using a small heater.
- Fans can help keep working temperatures more comfortable in summer.
- Move your desk away from windows if they are too draughty, or make you fry on hot, sunny days.
- Blinds and screens can help deal with problems created by both heat and draughts.

Check the temperature where you work and make any adjustments you can to feel more comfortable. Achieving an optimal room temperature can make a surprising difference – to you and your motivation.

Way 41 What others say

As John Donne said, 'No man is an Island, entire of itself'. If we were, perhaps the people we encounter in our daily lives would not affect us the way they do. Some make us feel good about life, ourselves, our work; others, that nothing is worth the effort.

When we're struggling to find the enthusiasm we need, the sort of people we mix with becomes even more important. Whether we want to be or not, we are influenced by other people's characters, so it won't help much to hang around people who like to do just that – hang around. The moaners, the despairers, the hard-done-bys, the how-awfuls, the can't-be-bothereds; give them all a wide berth. If you're already feeling less than inspired these people will only make things worse. Their company will reinforce your lack of motivation, not help overcome it. Avoid these people like the plague.

Conversely, hunt out the ones who are already fired with their own enthusiasm; the ones who enjoy their work whole-heartedly; the ones who see the blue sky, not the clouds on the horizon. These are the ones who will help you start to sense a glimmer of your own enthusiasm. Their energy will make you feel energetic, too. Their conversation will lift you up and make you feel ready to tackle things again. Search these people out as if your life depended on it!

If you're self-employed and surrounded by negative people the problem should be tackled with even more firmness. There is too much at stake to allow yourself to be dragged down by their unhelpful attitudes. They may have subconscious reasons for their behaviour and may even be trying to undermine your attempts at success. Jealousy of a partner's work is not unknown.

Spend a moment or two having an objective look at the people in your life. Do an inventory of those who make you feel good and those who don't. Make a pointed effort to spend more time with the former – and distinctly less with the latter. Your motivation could depend on it.

Way 42 Nutrient fuel

To be able to raise even the smallest amount of enthusiasm you have to feel good within. Being tired, run down, or feeling as though you're not quite firing on all four cylinders will make it that much harder. This is where vitamins and other micro-nutrients can play a vital role.

Many health professionals acknowledge that even eating

what we believe to be a healthy, balanced diet may not provide us with the level of nutrients our bodies require. This is due to how our food is produced and processed, our own eating habits, and the daily stresses to which we subject ourselves – just getting to work can be a major event in itself.

Consider these:

- Vitamin B complex, which affects the health of the nervous system, can become depleted when we're under stress. Insufficient amounts of this vitamin can lead to, among other things, increased levels of anxiety, depression and irritability.

- Vitamin C also becomes depleted when we're stressed out. This vitamin aids mental functioning.

- Potassium helps you stay sharp by making sure the brain receives enough oxygen.

- Manganese is said to improve memory.

- Insufficient iodine affects mental alertness.

- Iron helps the blood carry oxygen around the body. Without sufficient iron we simply can't operate efficiently either mentally or physically.

- Zinc promotes mental alertness.

- Magnesium also helps us cope when we're under stress.

- Amino acids play an important role in the psychological arena. They can affect mood swings, depression and anxiety, to name but a few.

Do exercise caution when taking any food supplements. Just because these micro-nutrients are perceived as being 'healthy' it does not mean they cannot be damaging if taken in inappropriate amounts. Check the labels and have a word with your GP if you are already on any other form of medication.

Getting the micro-nutrient balance right can bring about a real improvement in your sense of well-being. For further information, consult *Thorson's Complete Guide to Vitamins and Minerals* (1994) by Leonard Mervyn.

Way 43 One-minute wonder

Let's face it, there are some tasks we will never enjoy doing. Not even with a month of good days at our disposal will we find it easy to knuckle down to them. These are the ones which really test our ability to motivate ourselves.

With my own particular *bête noire*, I realised I could probably tolerate doing the task for one minute. A full 60 seconds. And although I still didn't relish the thought of it, I knew I could muster up enough energy for that small amount of time.

Using the kitchen timer again if need be (see Way 39) try settling down to do whatever job you've been putting off, for just one whole minute. When you've done that, congratulate yourself. Feel good about having made a start. See whether you can manage a repeat performance. If you think you can, do another minute; no longer, we don't want to overdo it and start to feel overwhelmed or demotivated again. If you don't feel up to another minute, put the job to one side, but make a note in your diary to do another minute in an hour's time. You might even set the timer to remind you.

Keep on taking these tip-toeing steps. Small they might be, but progress is still being made, providing a way in which to make a start on a task which otherwise might never happen.

Way 44 Slumping

If you're presently pondering your lack of motivation, without moving a muscle, make a note of how you are sitting: shoulders dropped, slumped in the chair, head hanging, leaning your head on your hand? These all indicate your less-than-perky attitude.

Now try sitting up straight, pulling your shoulders back into a relaxed position and lifting your head. Feel the difference? You should do. When we sit in a more upright position our circulation improves, our muscles relax into an easier pose, our ribcage opens up so that we breathe better. All in all, our bodies instantly start to work better when we sit properly. This in turn makes us feel better. And psychologically, when we sit up we look and feel more poised for positive action. It sends a message to our subconscious that we are ready for action.

If you work at home avoid drifting over to the easy chair; you're unlikely to find your motivation there. And if you're in it now, go and sit in your office or upright chair.

You might also check out your seating. It is vitally important to have a chair which is designed to support your body while you work, especially if you have a desk job. If your body is uncomfortable, it will be under stress and this will not only affect your energy levels but make you feel crabby as well. Get it changed.

By sitting properly you're not only helping your posture and preventing strains from developing, you're putting yourself in a state of readiness. Exactly the right attitude for starting to feel better about getting on with the work in hand.

Way 45 Raised glasses; lowered resolve

Reaching for a glass of something alcoholic in an attempt to lower the stress and anxiety which undone work provokes unfortunately has the same effect on our resolve to actually get on and do it. While we may have a few drinks with the aim of trying to bolster our enthusiasm, all it tends to do is take the sharp point off our conscience; the very thing which has been prodding us to take action. Too often a trip to the pub, bar or drinks cabinet is a futile attempt at trying to escape from it.

Alcohol is not an effective or even healthy way in which to try and motivate ourselves; in fact, quite the reverse. Alcohol is a depressant, which is why it makes people feel good initially – because it first acts to depress our inhibitions. This makes us act more lively and bubbly, giving us the mistaken impression that a 'sharpener' is just what we needed. Unfortunately, alcohol ultimately depresses our responses – and our energy levels. If enough is drunk it even sends us to sleep – hardly the right way to whip up enthusiasm for what needs doing.

Treat alcohol warily, especially at midday when most people feel the effects of it more acutely. Find other ways in which to relax or ease the strain if that is why you drink. A walk in the sunshine, taking in some fresh air will achieve just the same effect and leave you feeling refreshed, not sleepy and lethargic. If you feel you can't or don't want to avoid the pub at lunch times, switch to non-alcoholic wines or beers, join your companions later so you don't drink as much, or break with tradition and order a soft drink or coffee for a change. You might even set a new trend.

Use your favourite tipple as a reward instead. Promise yourself an indulgence *after* the work has been completed, *after* putting in the hours or *after* reaching a set target. Alcohol is enjoyable in moderation. As a reward it can help you get through the work on your table; used unwisely you might only end up under it.

Way 46 Help at every turn

Those days sometimes loom on the horizon which we know will be filled with chore after unending chore, or with one lengthy task which just can't be hurried. On days like this we need all the help we can get, and with just a little thought beforehand it is possible to turn the day into a more enjoyable, or at least more tolerable, experience.

Thinking about wading through the unending work, hour after hour, is not helpful and will only demotivate you. Don't focus on the drudgery of the task, but on the day as a whole. Think of how you can make it as enjoyable as possible and plan to give yourself a whole stream of pleasant treats and rewards from beginning to end:

- Start the day with a special breakfast treat, either at home, or by eating out – something Americans excel at.

- Wear your favourite outfit for the day so you feel good (see also Way 58).

- Surround yourself with pleasant things: a bunch of flowers; some pleasant aromas (see Way 17).

- Plan a schedule of background music, either quiet and soothing, stirring and upbeat, or a mix of the two.

- Arrange a special lunch time treat, preferably away from the office. You might even take in an art gallery or museum.

- Have something special to look forward to in the evening.

- Allow yourself to make a couple of (short) telephone calls to friends throughout the day.

- Treat yourself to a mid-afternoon cake if you're sure it won't affect your energy levels too much (check Way 38).

With days we know are going to be hard to get through, we need to keep the chores balanced out with just as many pleasant experiences. Next time you have one looming, take the time to plan it out so there is always something pleasant to be reminded of while you slave away instead of just the horrid work itself.

> 'If your work now gives you some joy and satisfaction you must cultivate it, just as you should cultivate everything that gives you some joy in being alive.'
>
> *Carl Jung*

Way 47 The worst first

When the 'Must Do' (sub-titled 'Don't Want To') list looks like defeating you before you start, try this well-known and successful strategy: do the worst thing on your list first.

Recoil in horror if you will at the mere suggestion of such a thing, but believe me, it works, and really can help motivate you to tackle the other items on your list with more gusto. It does mean you have to be a brave little bunny to deal with the first item, and you may have to integrate other strategies to help you cope (look at Ways 35, 39, 43, 44 or 64) but the pay-offs are worth it.

Working the other way round (completing the easiest first) doesn't work so well. All the time you whittle away at the other tasks, the Great One looms over you with its menacing presence. As the final confrontation moves ever closer, your willingness to complete any more jobs declines, since doing so will only bring you face to face with It.

Conversely, when you manage to complete the most onerous task first, you will feel such a sense of relief and accomplishment you'll be more inspired to dash off the other less irksome items on the list, more energised by striking such an early success, and more motivated all round.

Don't put yourself through torture by allowing unpleasant

tasks to hang around, menacingly, for extended lengths of time. Deal with them quickly. Get rid of them, pronto. You'll be so glad you did – you brave little bunny!

Way 48 Dilettante days

When you feel in a rut and the workaday routine starts weighing you down, or there's a list of chores to do, all equally uninspiring, think about having a dilettante day.

Although the word now tends to be used disparagingly to refer to someone who merely trifles with things, it originally stems from the Italian word for *delight*. A dilettante is one who delights in what they do or see. In the work context, having a dilettante day suggests combining these two meanings: flitting from one task to another, but finding delight in doing so.

Select, say, five pieces of work from the pile in front of you. Throughout the day, alternate between each of them every half-hour, or however long you wish. When the time is up, down tools and switch over to the next task, regardless of whether you have completed it or not. By working sporadically on each, none settle down into becoming an oppressive chore; and keeping all of them on the go means progress is continually being made on each.

Having a dilettante day brings a touch of lightness to otherwise gloomy lists of Things To Do. You may well find the regular changes stimulating and refreshing. Instead of ploughing through each boring chore, you can skitter from one to another. If you normally approach work in the same, tired old way, try treating yourself to a dilettante day instead.

Way 49 Get mad!

Just look at the work you have to do! Look at the dreadful tasks. I bet you hate them. They're boring. They're horrible. They're ghastly. How long have they been sitting there? Days? Weeks? Since last Bank Holiday? And do you want to do them any more now than you did then?

How much *don't* you want to do them? How much do you dislike them? How much? Surely you dislike them more than that. Let your real feelings of frustration towards them surface; let your anger towards their very existence fill you with rage. Let it bubble up and flood into your full consciousness. Let yourself get really mad about it all. Great! Now get even more angry with the stalemate and your profound inactivity. When you feel fit to burst with it all, let it out and let it propel you into action – perhaps quite radical action. In fact it might be so radical (are you ready for this?) that you even pick up that report, or whatever, and deal with it once and for all.

Getting really mad about your work may sound silly, but anger is an incredibly powerful emotion. It is potent enough to shift even the most reluctant procrastinator. Anger released can open the floodgates to access and release stores of energy you'll be surprised you had. There'll be more than enough to deal with whatever you've been dreading or putting off for so long.

Use this energy to fuel your motivation and propel you into activity. If nothing else will shift you, your anger might.

> 'If you have a job without aggravations, you don't have a job.'
>
> *Malcolm S Forbes*

Way 50 Forfeits

Shock tactics sometimes work. When motivation refuses to be roused, preferring instead to slumber away contentedly, reminding yourself of the real impact of allowing it to can have the effect of startling you into action.

Some minor tasks left undone may have few consequences but, even so, collectively they could cause real problems later on. For example, not filing away papers may seem unimportant enough – until you urgently need to put your hand on one of them. When tasks are left too long they can:

- Lead to delays.

- Lead to inefficiency.

- Make your job more frustrating.

- Actually *create* more work.

- Affect the quality of service to clients and customers.

- Create difficulties for, and with, colleagues.
- Affect levels of productivity.

Leaving major tasks, or those which form a core part of your job, undone can mean even greater forfeits. Procrastinating too long or too often can mean:

- Lost clients.
- Loss of good relations with line managers.
- Loss of free time spent having to catch up.
- Increased stress levels.
- Loss of promotion prospects.

It can even mean:

- Losing your job.

Think about what that would mean – for you, your family, and your prospects of securing another job. If you're self-employed, the penalties can be just as great. Ultimately it can lead to the loss of your business.

Yes, you can have another snack, but as you do so you're turning away from success. Yes, you can turn on the television or read the paper, but by doing so, you're failing to invest in your future. And yes, you can spend half an hour on the telephone chatting, but this may be blocking the sales call of the century.

Sometimes, especially if we're employed, it is easy to forget the consequences of our actions – or, in this case, non-action. Reflecting on the problems we are creating for ourselves and others, or on what we are denying ourselves by not getting down to it, reminds us of the very real consequences. The question to ask is whether you are willing to pay the price for putting off the work you *know* has to be done.

Way 51 Past perfect

One belief almost guaranteed to make anyone freeze up with fear is that a task should be done *perfectly*. The illustration must be flawless; the report worthy of a Nobel prize; the project plan total perfection. Such unattainable goals, well beyond the reach of mere mortals, are bound to hammer motivation levels into the ground and nail most of us to the psychological spot forever.

If this is currently your problem, think about what perfection means to you and your attitude to the task. What lofty heights are you mistakenly expecting yourself to reach? What do you erroneously perceive to be the rewards of completing the task perfectly? Now do a reality check:

- Are you a perfect human being? Highly unlikely, since the rest of us aren't.

- Who said you had to aim so high? Who is setting the unreachable standard? Probably yourself.

- Will anyone care much if you're a little wide of the perfection mark? Will people stop talking to you? Or do you secretly expect instant promotion to executive status if you do it perfectly? Get real. Basically, people couldn't give a damn: their expectations are set at a more realistic level, which means what you produce is likely to be well within their tolerance levels.

And what if the less-than-perfect work comes back to you? Well, you simply find out what adjustments need making – and make them. Simple. No end-of-the-world scenario. Just one or two tweaks and corrections.

Finding yourself stuck in a place of non-action is an uncomfortable experience. In order to move out of it, first check on the parameters for the task and clarify what your boss/client expects. You may be thinking they want more than in reality they do. If their expectations are unreasonable, say so and negotiate a more attainable target. Then resolve to do the job to the best of your abilities. Period. No god-like attainments; no miracle results; just hard graft within the bounds of what's expected and what you're capable of doing.

And with less important tasks, do them sloppily if need be – but for goodness' sake get them out of the way once and for all.

> 'An expert is a man who has made all the mistakes which can be made in a very narrow field.'
>
> *Niels Bohr*

Way 52 No, no, no

One of the most demotivating experiences to happen to anyone is failure or rejection. Its effect can carry far beyond the immediate let-down, and colour whatever comes afterwards. The knock to a person's confidence can make the prospect of new tasks seem even more daunting than it would normally. It's important to deal with disappointments if motivation is to flourish again. If possible, talk through the experience with a colleague and/or line manager. A colleague may be able to offer more sympathetic support and share their own, similar, experiences with you. A line manager, on the other hand, should help to debrief in a more objective way and facilitate a professional assessment of the situation.

In the process, line managers should identify with you what improvements, if any, could be made to avoid the same happening again. They should also assess whether a skills update or refresher course would be beneficial. In the fast-moving world of commerce change is ongoing, and it is easy to be left standing if your finger is off the pulse for a single beat.

If you're self-employed it is just as important to assess what went wrong – but without beating yourself up about it. Try to learn from what happened, and take any remedial action you feel is necessary: to your approach, product, pricing structure, target market, selling skills, or whatever.

Finally, it is also important to attach the rejection or failure label to the right thing – which is not yourself. What has failed is the attempt; what has been rejected is the approach; what is a disappointment is the outcome. You are none of those things.

Don't let an unwelcome result turn into a semi-permanent set-back. Learn what needs to be learned from the experience – and then let it go, because it's not until you do that you will find the energy and motivation to start moving forward again.

'God grant me the courage to change the things I can change, the serenity to accept the things I cannot change, and the wisdom to know the difference.'

St Francis of Assisi

Way 53 Time out

> 'Everyone knows that on any given day there are ener-
> gies slumbering in him which the incitements of that
> day do not call forth.'
>
> *William James*

We all recognise the importance of holiday times. Having a
break from regular work routines brings a breath of fresh air
into our lives, refreshes us and brings a welcome boost of
energy to our sorely depleted reserves. Unfortunately we
can't be off holidaying all the time, but the same principle
can be integrated into the times in between to help alleviate
the potentially demotivating effect of our humdrum existence. Work–television–sleep; work–shopping–sleep;
work–chores–sleep; work–television–sleep. If you recognise
this type of cycle the likelihood is that your overall level of
motivation could be running on empty.

Contrast, change, enjoyment, creativity, entertainment,
activity. Your non-work time should include at least some of
these on a regular basis. It shouldn't pass by in front of the
television every night of the week. Although sometime will
be taken up with chores, the rest of it including weekends,
should include enjoyable activities. A bit of pre-planning can
help start the ball rolling. Make a conscious effort to book
some of your favourite activities into the week ahead. Good
intentions don't count. Commit them to paper to remind
yourself that taking time out is as important as remembering
to do the laundry.

Keeping a balance to our lives can be a problem at times,
but if you're finding it difficult to maintain your levels of
motivation, taking time out to recharge the batteries could be
the answer. Go on; have some fun.

Way 54 Timed estimates

No matter how large or small the pile of tasks waiting to be
done, we tend to look at it as a whole, clump everything
together and refer to it as: work. Such an unwieldy, amor-

phous lump is bound to dishearten if our motivation isn't fired up good and strong. It can be overwhelming. Even if the pile isn't too large, when there seems to be a mismatch between it and our level of motivation, we're in trouble.

One way of dealing with this situation is to make the work seem more approachable by dividing it up into smaller pieces of a size to match our appetite for work. Do this by going through the pile of tasks and scribbling on each one how long you think it will take you to complete what needs doing. Larger tasks, which are likely to give you severe indigestion if you attempt them all in one go, can be broken down into smaller portions of say, 4 × 30 minutes; or 3 × 20 minutes. When you've done this you should be able to see not only how much time the work is likely to take, but you now have a menu of more bite-sized and palatable units of work to dip into. What may previously have seemed to be too much now looks more manageable. You've set targets which are more realistic.

Try this approach when you're feeling overwhelmed by what needs doing. When it's broken down into smaller units which match your level of motivation, you should find it easier to start making progress.

Way 55 Whittling

Whittling brings to mind pictures of old cowboys sitting on the back porch at night lazily shaving sticks down until there's nothing left. Nowadays it has come to mean slowly working away at any task, chipping away at it until it's all completed. And if you think about it, there's no reason why the idea of whittling can't be applied to tasks found in the more contemporary setting of your workplace.

A good time to whittle is at the end of the working day. Before packing up, do just five or ten minutes of filing or any other ongoing task which somehow you keep failing to find the time (ie motivation) to do. Eventually you'll find the pile miraculously disappears.

The end of the working week is also a good whittling time. When your enthusiasm and energy for your main work is starting to ebb and you find yourself staring off into space, have a quick whittle. A change of tempo is often welcome at times like this, so put your other work to one side and spend a few minutes on a different task, perhaps one which has been hanging around for way too long.

Instead of waiting for the 'right time', or trying to find enough motivation to get particular jobs out of the way in one go, try whittling. It might turn into a pleasant diversion in itself.

Way 56 The long and winding road

In order to maintain levels of motivation it is important to have some sort of recognition or acknowledgement of our progress – the proverbial pat on the back. Without it one can too easily end up in the doldrums – everything seems routine, and work becomes lacklustre. This is when motivation is in danger of slackening off. 'Too late,' you may say, 'It's already started to leave.'

Good employers make time, at least once a year, to hold regular reviews with staff for this very purpose. These also provide an opportunity to identify difficulties, set new targets and iron out any problems. If this is missing in your situation, consider approaching your line manager to see if they would be willing to instigate such a procedure. If they aren't, or you are self-employed and don't have anyone to give you the feedback you need, the next best thing is to do it yourself – not as impossible a task as it might seem.

Look back over the last six months or year. Pick out your major achievements; tot up the money you've earned – for yourself and the company; list new clients found; amount of stock moved; projects completed. Include as many items as you want which indicate the degree of progress you've made over the time period you're looking at. You may be surprised – and cheered – when you see the cumulative totals and list of achievements to date. You have every right to feel proud of what you have accomplished.

Done regularly, this simple exercise should help keep your overall motivation levels on a more even keel – and help restore them whenever you feel they've gone walkabout.

Way 57 Don't do it

When we have the prospect before us of work we positively

want to do, lack of motivation tends not to raise its problematic head. It's when we are facing jobs we *don't* want to do that motivation does its disappearing act. Although most of the other Ways address how to find that missing motivation, this one will really make you sit up and take notice.

Startling though it might seem, on occasion it is a valid strategy to make a positive decision not to do the work at all. That's right. Cross it off the list. Give it the boot. Take it out of the equation, and don't do whatever is causing problems for you. Obviously, this strategy can't be applied all the time or else we'd soon find ourselves in deep trouble, but when used with discretion it can be as appropriate a way as any other in which to deal with something which is causing us difficulties.

To decide whether it is the best course of action, consider the following:

- Is the work essential?
- What would the *full* consequences be of not doing the task?
- How would you deal with the consequences?
- What would the benefits be of not doing the work?
- What would be the full consequences of doing it? In the long term, would it be more beneficial to knuckle down and do the work than not?

If you feel you could handle the consequences of not doing the work, and that there are as many benefits to be had by not doing it as going ahead, then crossing it off your list might be the best course of action. On the other hand, if the knock-on effect for either customers/clients, colleagues or yourself would be too great then forget the idea; but when considering other people, don't automatically assume they could not cope with, or would not welcome, a change of plan. Talk things over with them. They may come up with some useful suggestions.

Deciding not to do a task is often overlooked as a strategy, but when done mindfully it can sometimes prove to be the best solution. Don't act hastily, but take time to consider whether on this occasion *not doing it* would be your best course of 'action'.

> 'Work is the great cure of all maladies and miseries that ever beset mankind.'
>
> *Thomas Carlyle*

Way 58 Dress for the job

A lot can be deduced from a person's dress. To a greater or lesser degree it can reflect how they feel on that particular day; the type of job they do; their status; what sort of person they are. Equally, how we dress can affect how we feel. Some outfits make us feel better about ourselves, while others make us feel uncomfortable and 'not right' every time we wear them.

Taking this knowledge one step further, clothes can be used to help us feel more ready to tackle those jobs we may be finding it difficult to settle down to. For example, since I work at home I normally dress fairly casually but, when I have to do something I don't like doing (accounts being one), I dress differently. Instead of jeans and a top I dress in accountancy mode, ie a smart, formal skirt suit, complete with office shoes. The hair goes up; the make-up goes on.

No one sees me dressed this way; it is purely for my own benefit to put me in the correct frame of mind for the work I have to do. I am dressed for some serious, organised desk work so I feel ready to tackle those sorts of tasks. If I stay in jeans and sweatshirt I simply don't feel 'geared up' for dealing with cash flows, budgets and taxes.

I also use this tactic when I simply need to make sure I have a particularly productive day. Dress me in leggings and a T-shirt and you'll find me lolling around instead. Put me in executive clothes and I start to act the part.

If there is less opportunity to change your dress, work within the limitations you have. Dressing as casually as you would do at home for the hard graft awaiting you may not be possible, but think about how your outfit could be modified to make it feel more comfortable. Similarly, if you already dress smartly but need a boost to tackle the day, wear your favourite outfit or one you normally reserve for job interviews.

Changing how we dress won't make tasks any more pleasant, but it can help you feel better in yourself about being able to tackle them. Try it and see.

Way 59 Coffee break, tea break

Having a coffee or tea break is very different from simply having a cup of tea or drinking a cup of coffee. At work we may do plenty of the latter, but never actually take a break from one day's end to the other. No wonder we end up feeling worn out or as though we are grinding on without any gusto to speak of.

We need proper breaks from work. We need short periods to down tools, walk away from it all and allow our minds a short breathing space in which to change gear. When we take a proper break we allow our minds to come up for air, so to speak, and recharge the batteries which have become depleted while applying ourselves so assiduously to what needs doing.

People who don't take breaks but simply have cups of coffee at their desks while continuing to work are more likely to wear themselves out, kill off any enthusiasm they may have had to begin with, and even end up plain bored. In the short term, missing a tea break won't matter, but when we consistently treat ourselves like a workhorse we are bound to wear ourselves out – and that's when it will become difficult to rally the motivation we need. We'll simply be too exhausted.

So try to get into the regular habit of taking a proper break from your work. Go and sit somewhere away from your desk – even if it means sitting at someone else's or just staring out of the window. Don't take any work with you or read anything directly connected with it. Literally, give yourself a break. You'll feel much better for it.

Way 60 Psyche me up, Scotty

Good managers regularly give words of encouragement to their staff. Some companies even make it their policy to give pep talks at the start of every day. And we've all seen athletes being talked up by their trainers to help them succeed. Perhaps the rest of us could benefit from hearing a few uplifting words now and then, too.

In the absence of having someone whose duty it is to encourage us, we should take on the task ourselves and indulge in some positive self-talk to psyche ourselves up, ready to achieve. This may be a far cry from what you normally say to yourself, especially when fretting over getting down to work which you don't want to do. Thoughts tend to be about how awful the work is; how terrible you feel; how much you don't want to do it; how much of it there is to do. It's all negative, full of 'don'ts', 'can'ts', 'awfuls' and problems – words unlikely to inspire.

Try instead to change the words you say to yourself into something more positive. Imagine you are that manager giving words of encouragement to staff, psyching up a whole team of people to go out there and win. What would you say? How would you make it upbeat? Which words would act like magic to inspire them to achieve? These are the words you need to say to yourself. This is what you need to hear to encourage you, to lift your motivation, to renew your determination to successfully deal with the tasks ahead.

Make a recording of this speech, deliver it to yourself in front of a mirror, or simply run through it quietly in your own mind. The important thing is to replace the negative, self-defeating phrases which normally dominate with positive, motivational ones. Hearing a few words of encouragement, albeit your own, may be all you need.

> 'Nothing great was ever achieved without enthusiasm.'
> *Ralph Waldo Emerson*

Way 61 Put yourself on the line

Day after day I can make a thousand promises to myself crammed with all the good intentions I like, and if I don't achieve even one of them no one else is any the wiser. They won't know I intended to write 3000 words today but instead watched the afternoon film on television. They won't have a clue I planned to tackle that Pisa-like tower of filing but instead went for a walk in the park. No one knows, so what does it matter if things are left undone? Trying to be our own taskmaster and answer to ourselves can be an almost impossible task in itself.

To overcome this dilemma, try telling someone else of your plans. Let them know your intentions for the day or week, or about how you are going to tackle the outstanding work. Tell them your targets and goals. Make them realistic, not only for your own benefit, but so that you don't come across as though you are bragging, or just 'full of it'. People won't take you seriously if you don't sound genuine.

Once you've let others know your plans, you'll probably find they'll follow it up and ask whether you've managed to complete what you said you would. You'll be put on the (embarrassing) spot if you have to own up to failure – in public. This salutary experience should be enough to toughen your resolve to get things done.

No one likes to be seen to fail, but while we keep our intentions to ourselves no-one is any the wiser. Telling others of your plans may be the motivational stick you need to make sure you do what you've been promising yourself – perhaps for far too long.

Way 62 Mentors

For some people, work can be an isolating experience. Those in positions of responsibility may have few to confide in; those from minority groups may feel the same; the self-employed often cite this as a problem. It can happen to anyone who finds themselves working alone or alongside colleagues with whom they have little in common other than sharing the same employer. It can also happen to anyone who has a specialist job or who fulfils an unpopular role; they too may find the going tough.

Isolation can affect motivation. We know from Maslow's theory that being recognised and acknowledged by people is a basic need. We need relationships which confirm our sense of belonging. Being with others with whom we share a professional common bond stimulates us. Without it we can end up feeling like we're working in a vacuum. Starved of air, it can leave our motivation gasping on the floor like a landed fish.

Finding a mentor is one way of filling the gap. A mentor is normally someone who works in the same or a similar field and with whom one can share experiences. In mentoring programmes within companies, the mentor is often a more senior person who can offer guidance as well. Think about someone you know who might be willing to act as your mentor. It might be someone within the company, or another professional working elsewhere. It might be an acquaintance with whom you could operate a reciprocal arrangement, or a close friend or relative might fit the bill. Explain what you need from them in the mentoring role: to take a positive (as opposed to polite) interest in what you are doing; to listen to problems; to share your successes, and commiserate with your failures. Advice may be the last thing you want. It's up to you. When you've found the right person, agree how often to meet or contact each other.

Having a mentor in your working life could help fill a gap in the support structure which we all need to keep us going. Talk through the idea with a few people. If professional isolation is a factor affecting your motivation, a mentor might provide the answer you need.

Way 63 Affirmations

When our motivation sinks, positive thoughts don't get a look in. Instead, we turn into worrywarts and fret about the battle we know lies ahead of us with work we'd rather avoid or simply can't find the wherewithal to do. Once we're in this negative frame of mind it can be difficult to break out of it. This is where affirmations can help.

Affirmations are short, positive statements spoken to yourself. When said often enough and with conviction they reprogramme ways of thinking by replacing those unhelpful thoughts which keep us stuck. From a thought follows action. It may not be immediate, but to change the way we act (or don't, in this case) we first need to change the initial thought. Telling ourselves over again how little we want to do a job is hardly likely to inspire positive action; but telling ourselves how ready we are to tackle the task will.

Affirmations are simple to construct. They must be short, positive and in the present tense. For example:

• I feel strong and positive.

- I am ready and eager for work.
- I enjoy the challenge my work provides.
- The energy I need to do the work is already within me.
- I have a wellspring of determination/creativity/ability.

Make up affirmations to suit your own situation. Remember, keep them short to be effective and keep them positive – state what you aspire to, not what you don't. For example, 'I don't avoid these tasks', won't work. Change it to, 'I approach my work with determination'. Also remember to keep it in the present tense as though it is already happening. What use is wording it in the future ('I *will* enjoy my work') when you're in the here and now?

Repeat your affirmations throughout the day. Pay attention to the words as you say them quietly to yourself. Let their message filter through to your subconscious. Used properly, you should find affirmations a useful tool in helping to give your motivation a welcome extra boost.

Way 64 As if

Hamlet advised, 'Assume a virtue, if you have it not'. Acting as if you already have the qualities you feel are lacking is a useful game plan when motivation is otherwise reluctant to surface.

Spend a few moments thinking about the way in which you would make the phone calls you've been avoiding *if* you could handle them successfully. Imagine what you would be like tackling the tasks you've been putting off *if* you felt motivated to do them. Bring to mind how you might feel *if* you were actually doing any job or task which you have been finding it difficult to make a start on.

Once you have it clear in your mind what you would be like and how you would be handling the tasks which lie before you, go ahead and *act as if* you were. You might still not like doing the filing, but act *as if* you do. You might still quake as you pick up the phone to make the call you've been dreading, but act *as if* you are confident, self-assured and successful. Really believe it – even if it is only for as long as it takes to do the job. Send out the message to other people that you are capable, dynamic and motivated and they will see you in that way; but it needs to start with you sending the same message to yourself.

Acting *as if*, like affirmations, helps to reprogramme negative attitudes. If we keep telling ourselves we'll never get the work done, or ever feel motivated, we won't. Acting as if you are the most self-motivated creature ever to walk God's earth may be nothing more than make-believe, but who's to know? And if it gets you moving again, who cares?

Way 65 Training for the big event

'I just can't make myself do it;' 'I can't seem to bring myself to get on with it.' It's as if our willpower is like some reluctant child, stubborn mule or mutinous crew. When it comes to facing up to the enormous task in front of us we balk and mentally turn our backs on it. Too late, we realise our willpower has turned into some contrary beast with a mind of its own. Bringing it back in line means training it to start working as an ally again. This means exercising control over it, starting with small, non-threatening tasks; ones not even necessarily found in the workplace.

Start by checking yourself when you walk past a cup which needs taking to the kitchen; the pair of socks which should be put in the laundry; the towel which should be picked up off the floor. They are only small, almost insignificant items, but when we catch ourselves not dealing with them we are letting our willpower become even more lax and flabby. Start addressing other minor tasks which you keep turning away from. They could be enjoyable ones: the film you've been meaning to see; the friend you've been meaning to catch up with; the time you've been meaning to spend on your favourite hobby.

Keep practising exercising your willpower. Find small ways in which to reinforce your mastery and control over it. Hopefully, soon you should find it becoming more pliable and less rebellious – a perfect ally once again.

> 'What we have to learn to do, we learn by doing.'
> *Aristotle*

Way 66 A period of adjustment

Setting goals is important to ensure we continue to make progress in our daily lives. When we know where we are heading, our energies can be more easily focused.

The goals we set should be a continuous source of motivation, but problems can arise if they are set at inappropriate levels. If every time you turn your mind to what needs doing your motivation sinks like an expired balloon, it may be time to have a look at your goals afresh. Take a look at particular problem areas. Look at them in the light of the goals they represent and the factors which may be affecting their appeal. Reasons can include:

- *Too difficult a target*. Goals need to be achievable in order for them to motivate.

- *Not enough time* to complete the task. Too much pressure can demotivate.

- *Not enough resources* to support your efforts. This too can be demotivating.

- *Not enough enthusiasm* for the project. It may be one which never really sparked your enthusiasm.

- *Not enough challenge*. Goals set too low may not provide sufficient levels of motivation.

- *You've changed*. You may have new skills, new priorities, new interests.

- *No longer appropriate*. Circumstances change which can mean a project loses its validity.

Consider the goals you are striving to work towards and ask yourself whether they are serving to motivate. Reassess whether they are relevant to you and where you want to go. If not, look at what can be done to change them. Renegotiate with line managers, clients and/or partners if need be. Few things in life are set in stone.

Times change. People change. If what you are aiming for no longer provides the motivation you need, it may be time to change the goal itself.

Way 67 Working smarter, not harder

It is when work reaches fever pitch and we feel like we're swimming against the tide that our motivation often packs its bags and decides it's time for a break. Perhaps it's trying to tell us something.

Working harder may not always be the best long-term solution to those increased pressures at work which are more than just temporary blips. This is particularly true for people who are self-employed. A point can come when realisation dawns that no more hours can possibly be squeezed out of the day no matter how one tries, or more customers found for a product not enough people want. Working harder then fails to become an option which means either standing still or having a bad situation grow worse. Under these circumstances, working smarter is the only sensible answer.

Working smarter will mean different things in different situations, and depend on whether you're employed or self-employed, but these suggestions may provide clues as to how you might improve your situation:

- Increase your charges.
- Hire staff.
- Use outworkers.
- Sub-contract work.
- Delegate more.
- Renegotiate your job description.
- Invest in time-saving equipment.
- Change the way you handle projects.
- Negotiate for an assistant.
- Investigate how new technology might help.

Work levels need to be achievable if they are to motivate rather than simply overwhelm, and progress should not mean working ourselves into a corner. If the situation feels as though it may be getting the better of you, have a brainstorming session (Way 16) and see if you can come up with some novel solutions of your own which will allow you to start working smarter, not harder.

Way 68 The power of doing nothing

It may come as a surprise to find in a book about motivating yourself a suggestion which advises doing nothing but, paradoxically, it can work, according to time management expert Alan Lakein.

Doing nothing is not the same as crossing an unpleasant item off your list. It simply means sitting without doing anything; no displacement activity, no reading, not even thinking about what you should be seeing to. Sit with the full knowledge that the work is not being done. It's like deciding to hold a showdown, the final confrontation, right there in your office. It's you or your work; your procrastination or your motivation. Which one will win?

What you may initially find while sitting there resolutely not lifting a finger is a sense of relief: you're not doing the work and neither are you fretting over it. Peace at last. You've stepped out of the battle zone. After a while however, a certain degree of discomfort might begin to settle over you again. You may start getting a bit twitchy; perhaps wanting to reach for the telephone to start making calls, or read that piece of paper hanging halfway out of the in-tray. Resist. Do nothing. Try to keep your mind and body as still as possible.

One of two things could then happen. If you've been able to keep your mind clear enough, a new insight into your difficulty with work may suddenly pop into your mind unannounced. Sitting quietly gives your subconscious mind uninterrupted time to get to work on processing new solutions. Alternatively, unable to bear the inactivity any longer and at last seeing how futile it is to waste time doing nothing, you'll probably find yourself setting to with renewed vigour.

With today's focus on productivity we can sometimes overlook the ground to be gained by doing nothing. When your motivation seems long dead and buried, try this strategy and see what happens. Doing nothing could be what you needed to do all along.

Way 69 A pleasure awaits

We can be so harsh on ourselves at times. We assume it is enough that we receive a financial reward for doing the work in hand: the salary at the end of the month or the cheque from paying customers. Yet the direct link between what we do and the reward given is often lost due to the time which passes in between. Each completed task goes by without our thinking we should give any special recognition to ourselves for having completed it.

Giving ourselves rewards is important in maintaining healthy levels of self-motivation. This is particularly important if you work for yourself. An employee may have a good line manager to give regular praise, one form of reward, but when you're working for yourself this often doesn't happen. Rewards give a boost when they are unexpected, but they can also be used as something to look forward to; another aim separate from the other goals you're working towards.

Think about the rewards you might integrate into your way of working, especially if you have unpleasant tasks waiting to be done. They can help provide something more pleasant on which to focus rather than the chore itself. Rewards needn't be expensive, or even cost anything at all. It might be a special half-hour break; a browse through an article you've been wanting to read; a chat with a colleague over coffee. Whatever rewards seem appropriate, use them consciously to help you work through your task, not as an afterthought.

We all work hard at our jobs and, hopefully, most of us receive an appropriate remuneration for doing so, but we might all benefit from remembering to be kinder to ourselves by choosing and using other rewards as well; ones more directly linked to each task. Motivation is like a puppy dog; reward it regularly with treats and it'll keep its little tail wagging for a long time to come. Make sure you give yours enough.

Way 70 The great undone

Making a start on the day's work can often be problematic. Summoning the energy to launch into a new task is where many come to a stumbling halt. It can feel like too big a challenge, and so we start dilly-dallying around; wasting time when we could be making good headway.

A way around this morning start problem can be found by reducing the size of the hurdle itself. Since the difficulty is often in making an attempt at a new task, of breaking through into virgin territory, try to avoid it happening in the first place. Ensure you don't have to start afresh first thing.

The way to do this is by leaving a task or project uncompleted the day before. Normally we aim to tie things up before we go home, which may make for a tidy finish but means the next morning starts with the daunting prospect we're trying to avoid. It is much easier to sit down and pick up where you left off. After refreshing your memory about the point you reached it is like coming up to speed in double-quick time. Without much effort you're already part-way through a task, making you feel like you've already achieved. Your motivation loves it. It perks up cheerily, and sets you off to a flying start.

Try paying attention to the point at which you decide to leave jobs each day. Having even a small part to complete the following day will mean you start the morning achieving at once – a more positive start you couldn't wish for.

Way 71 What a picture!

When we're doing battle with our motivation we need all the help we can find. Often the reward system works, or receiving words of encouragement. But there are other triggers which can also usefully serve to reinforce our resolve and motivation when they threaten to dwindle away.

Visual images can be potent triggers. A picture of somewhere you're saving up to visit provides a concrete reminder of the goals you're working towards. Or it may be a car, new home, or replacement sound system. An image of whatever you're striving for can be used to renew your determination to succeed.

Other images may be less materialistic but work just as well. Photographs of loved ones can remind you of the time you want to spend with them, unfettered by worries about uncompleted work. They may remind you of the provision you want to make for them. Or they may simply inspire you just by looking at them. Photographs of role models can also help. Images of awards you're aiming for; premises you want to move your business to; companies you're working towards winning over as clients. Choose images which really mean something important to you.

Words can also motivate. Quotes, poems, articles, any written piece which inspires every time you read it can help to bring a speedy lift when you start to go downhill. And don't forget affirmations (Way 63). Reading them as written words works as well as simply saying them to yourself.

Surrounding our work spaces with meaningful images can be a simple way in which to build a supportive environment for ourselves. Start collecting images which fire your enthusiasm. A glance in their direction can help give another little boost to your motivation, perhaps just when you need it most.

Way 72 If the carrot doesn't work...

We're working in an age when job security is a fragile and scarce commodity. Whether we're employed or self-employed, the spectre of being unemployed is a reality of which we're all only too well aware. Once out of a job many find it difficult to find their way back into another.

When motivation stubbornly refuses to budge, see whether being reminded of the situation provides a big enough stick to wave at yourself. See if the threat of redundancy, bankruptcy or being sacked is enough to urge you on. If you're self-employed, think about the repercussions of having your enterprise fold through not getting on with your work – not least of which may mean having to get a job and work for someone else again. Horrors! Or you could become bankrupt, be taken to court, and have to pay damages for not completing agreed works. And just think of all the hard work you've put into building up your business going to waste – just because you let things slip. If you're in a job, think of all the difficulties you would have to face if you lost it: the loss of income, the hassle of applying for interviews, the problems it would create for your family. The anguish created by that situation is surely far worse than the discomfort of dealing with an unpleasant task or two and getting them out of the way.

Pondering on this bottom line can be a salutary experience. If you really dislike every aspect of your job then moving on would be no bad thing, but if you've simply been putting off for too long making a start on whatever needs doing, thinking about the reality of not having a job to moan about could help put those tasks in a new perspective.

Way 73 My sweet

Without realising it you may be sabotaging your own attempts at self-motivation. Eating sugary foods is the culprit. They can have a devastating overall effect on energy levels even though they may provide a short-lived instant lift and mislead you into thinking they are just what you needed. Yet without sufficient and sustainable energy at your disposal, drumming up enough motivation to get on with work can be nigh on impossible.

The problem with sweets and chocolates is that the high sugar content they contain is rapidly absorbed by our bodies (giving us the lift we enjoy), but as a result of the insulin released in order to cope with the sugar intake we then experience a compensatory energy drop. The lift which the bar of chocolate provides soon fades, leaving us feeling more tired than before. It's as if the excessive sugary overload were treated like an alien – and in some respects it is. Our internal mechanisms aggressively try to remove it from the system to bring glucose levels in our blood back to within more tolerable limits. Treating ourselves to the occasional chocolate won't do much harm, but consuming too much sugar over a long period of time can also deplete the body of important nutrients like chromium. Insufficient amounts of this mineral can affect not only the blood sugar balance, but also emotional and mental stability.

Maintaining a good energy balance is key in order to prevent fatigue from developing and affecting your motivation. There are healthier ways in which to keep the furnace burning rather than tearing through one chocolate bar after another. If you think sugar overload might be part of your problem in being able to drum up the energy to motivate yourself, start cutting back, and read Way 38, 'Energy foods'.

Way 74 Working cooperatively

Brave little souls that we are, we often struggle on courageously at our individual desks, isolated from each other by the dictates of our personal workloads. We try to soldier on but sometimes the motivational well runs completely dry. At times like these, instead of battling on alone we could try turning to each other for the help we need.

Working cooperatively with others is not something we tend to think of doing, unless it is the standard work practice or a special arrangement for dealing with a particular project; yet much strength can be gained from sharing our workloads with others.

Have a chat with one or more colleagues about the tasks they find onerous. A number of possible solutions might present themselves:

- Swapping tasks – John quite enjoys filing, which you hate, and will happily swap in exchange for updating his database.

- All hands on deck – everyone agrees to work together on someone's task to help them speed it out of the way.

- Working together – agreeing to set aside a special time so that everyone works on their own irksome tasks together.

- Support staff – if there is enough evidence to support it, suggest an assistant is hired to deal with those tasks which hold everyone back.

You may be able to come up with some other suggestions between you.

For people who are self-employed, teaming up with others who work in the same field might solve what can be more severe problems with isolation. Sharing the same office or other work space; teaming up to work on projects; or making it a more formal co-operative or partnership arrangement are all options worth considering.

Keeping our work boundaries wrapped too tightly around us is often not as necessary as we imagine it to be. Working cooperatively and learning to support each other can be an excellent way to motivate not only ourselves but our colleagues as well.

Way 75 Fear of success

It can be startling to discover that, far from helping ourselves along, we do things which keep us rooted to the spot, unwilling to move forward, yet unable to let go. We may believe it is a simple case of lack of motivation but at the root of it could be something more complex. Persistent failure to make any breakthroughs, to take a grip on what needs doing, or make any real headway can, surprisingly, sometimes be down to a fear not of failure, but of success.

Spend some time thinking about what it would mean to you if you were to solve all those problems concerning work which seem to be affecting your motivation, or manage to find a way of dealing with the tasks which you feel hold you back. Would you feel free, released, and able to pursue your potential to the full? Or, if you're honest with yourself, would you then come up against some other underlying problems? These fears might revolve around:

- Changing the balance of relationships.

- Losing your dependence on others.

- Finding that without your worries there would be nothing else to occupy your mind – or your life.

- Fear of alienating people.

- Becoming like your mother/father/sibling.

- Discovering your dreams don't bring you the joy you imagined they would.

Start being honest with yourself about the fears which lurk beneath the surface of your own personal image of success. Unless you start to confront whatever you imagine lies ahead, terrorising you every time you think about moving closer to it, you will stay put, wondering why you don't have the motivation you feel you should.

Way 76 Beat the clock

'Chi Wen Tzu always thought three times before taking action. Twice would have been quite enough.'

Confucius

We know how crucial setting goals is in helping us to make progress with our work. Besides the more long-term aims, time can also be used as an effective motivator – and even introduce a game-like element to the job of wading through accumulations of work.

Set a time goal of, say, one hour in which to clear your 'To Do' list of tasks which you've been putting off for too long. If you need a longer time period in which to deal with things, include time for a short break part-way through; there's no point overdoing it and ending up demotivated again. You may also want to put calls on hold for the time allotted so you won't be distracted.

Make sure your goal contains enough of a challenge. If you allow yourself an hour to complete a job which really should take just ten minutes you'll no doubt end up wasting the other 50. Similarly, trying to squeeze two hours of work into 30 minutes will only succeed in demotivating. To make sure you stick to your target, arrange for another activity to take place at the end of the allocated time period. It might be a meeting with a colleague or visit to a client. This helps to reinforce the importance of completing the task(s) on time.

And don't forget about rewards, too (Way 69). A self-administered pat on the back in recognition of your achievement will make you feel even better for having managed to succeed in clearing the work away at last. Motivation responds well to a challenge if it is set at an appropriate level. Using time goals may be just the way to do it.

Way 77 A little bit of help

'How can I take an interest in my work when I don't like it?'

Francis Bacon

People who run their own business may be skilled in graphic design or management consultancy but they also have to take on board duties which, in a larger company, are normally handled by others. This can mean an enormous workload. Not only does the work have to be completed for paying clients but a whole host of other ancillary tasks have to be dealt with as well. Without careful management it is all too easy to feel overwhelmed and demotivated by it all. Using professionals is key (Way 11), but there are other ways of finding additional help which won't cost the earth.

Make a list of chores – ones which require no special skills but which need to be attended to on a regular basis. Filing, doing mail-shots, distributing leaflets, checking stationery, posting letters, cleaning the car, and so on. All time-consuming but essential tasks which take you away from clients' work. Now think about people who might be able to lend a helping hand:

- A neighbour who would welcome a break from the children.
- A school or college leaver wanting to build up their work experience.
- Young family members in exchange for a boost to their pocket money.
- A student wanting to supplement their meagre grant.
- Someone recovering from a long absence from employment who would welcome the chance to get back in the swing of things again.
- Friends and relatives.
- Someone who finds retirement leaves them with too much time on their hands.

With just a few hours of willing assistance and an extra pair of hands to rely on you could find your motivation soon starts to blossom once again, so look around and see who might be able to offer *you* a little bit of help.

Way 78 Working in harmony

Clocks – and society's norms – tend to dictate when we do a lot of things in life. At 9 am we are generally supposed to be ready to start work, whether physical or mental. At 1 pm we are expected to be ready for a break and have our appetite primed. Our energy and concentration span is supposed to last us through until the clock tells us we can stop and go home. What this timetable doesn't take into account is our individual ebbs and flows of energy throughout the day.

Even so, there is much that can be done to improve the situation within the constraints of the working environment. Start by monitoring and becoming familiar with your own peaks and troughs. Make a note of when you:

- Find mental work easiest to do.

- Find physical tasks easiest.

- Feel most hungry.

- Feel energy levels take a dip.

- Need a break – every hour or every few minutes.

- Feel less talkative.

- Feel more communicative, and so on.

Once you are aware of your existing natural inclinations it is easier to start working with them, not against them. For example, if you find you are ravenously hungry by 11 am, see if you can arrange to take an early lunch. This means you will be fuelling your body when it needs it most instead of hoping it will get by on another snack bar. If you feel most talkative mid-afternoon make sure you plan phone calls or meetings for that period – not when you normally feel a grunt is all you can manage.

Also take note not just of daily rhythms but of weekly, monthly and even yearly ones. With a little careful planning it's possible to work more in harmony with both the dictates of the clock *and* our own natural rhythms. When this happens you should find your productivity improves – and your motivation.

Way 79 The big question

You might feel your problem with motivation goes deeper than just the one or two tasks you find difficult or irksome to do. Your procrastination may have done more than just hit a bad (or is it good?) patch. Your lack of motivation may seem to colour your days from one gloomy week to another rather than just for the occasional afternoon. That's OK. It happens. But when it does, it may call for some hard thinking.

If you can't see the possibility of things improving then take a look at what your lack of motivation is trying to tell you. It could be that it's time for a change. A big change. And the big question has to be asked: is your job really for you? It may be that your present job has reached the end of its life cycle. You may have loved it once, but things change. People change. You may be ready for a new challenge, a new environment, even a new career.

Before you go rushing into the boss's office waving your letter of resignation, think about whether other, less dramatic, changes could be made. A refresher course, training for promotion, negotiating a change in your job description, putting in for a transfer. Investigate and consider all the options available to you. It may help to talk to someone from personnel, your line manager, or a professional advisor.

It could be that, after all the soul-searching, all you really need is a long holiday, but if asking the big question made you realise that more fundamental changes are needed, so be it. We are dynamic beings and need the right sort of stimulus to make us feel alive. If your present job can no longer provide it then starting to look for a new one may be your best course of action.

> 'Everyone is dragged on by their favourite pleasure.'
>
> *Virgil*

Way 80 Out of harm's way

Although we may say we want to find the motivation to do our work, something inside often seems to pull us back, stops us from moving forward, keeps us stuck in one place. This *blocking* or *reluctant* part of ourselves can be pretty powerful; a seemingly invincible foe in the battle for your drive and enthusiasm.

In order to move forward, the part of us which tries to block our every attempt needs to be dealt with. One strategy I've found useful is to imagine this other self as a sort of cardboard cut-out, shield or sheet of plywood. It stands between me and the work in front of me – in my case, the computer screen. Mentally, I imagine picking up this blockage and gently but firmly putting it to one side. Sometimes it tries to slide back across, so you may have to be quite assertive with it, but once it's out of the way it's much easier to get down to work.

Another way of dealing with blockages is to listen to what your 'blocking self' has to say. Perhaps it is frightened, needs reassurance or is trying to tell you something useful. Find a quiet moment and imagine your blocking self sitting in the chair opposite. Have a chat with it. Hear it out. If it wants reassurances, give them. Explain what you want to achieve and get it to agree to help. This may sound weird, but it is an established therapeutic approach. Try it.

Other ways include more involved procedures: meditating and imagining an object or being which represents your blocks, then dissolving it to make it disappear.

When you suffer from blockages which are interfering with being able to make progress with your work, learning how to put them out of harm's way can be a powerful tool in helping to unleash the motivation you've been striving to find.

Way 81 People fix

Getting a 'people fix' level to suit our individual preferences can be difficult. Too much time spent chatting can be frustrating, tiring and all too easy a reason for procrastinating. Too little and one of our basic needs, human contact, is left wanting. Feelings of isolation can be most debilitating – and demotivating – so getting the levels right is important, particularly for people who are self-employed.

Learning to be more assertive solves the problem of too many people, but making more contact with others needs effort of a different kind, involving thinking and planning.

First, think about where you might meet others in your field. Make a special effort to attend training courses, seminars and conferences. Join professional and trade associations, and business or related interest groups. Draw up a schedule of meetings so you always have something to look forward to. Apart from the benefits on the professional front, it provides the opportunity to make new acquaintances who then serve to boost the list of those you can include in your 'people fix' network.

At the informal level, make sure you regularly arrange to meet with other colleagues. A standing arrangement might suit best. It's too easy to let another month pass by without making contact. You might also want to consider linking up with a few like-minded others and agree to contact each other regularly – perhaps daily, even if it is only by telephone, e-mail or fax. Even this helps to maintain a bridge to the 'outside world'.

Getting the 'people fix' you need is vitally important to stay motivated. Look at your needs and see what changes you could introduce to get the balance right.

Way 82 Working authentically

If we're having to do battle with ourselves, on any front, finding our motivation is bound to be an uphill task. One such battle can occur when we find our work, or an aspect of it, in conflict with our own personal belief system, or our own personal mission in life.

Many top companies now adopt a mission statement which sets out their aims and what they aspire to as a business. We may not have anything quite so formal but we all know when our outer world is in harmony with what is right for us, or what we believe is good and proper. When it doesn't we know straightaway from the discomfort and unsettled feelings we experience. That's often when our motivation moves out.

Think about what you are doing, or being asked to do, as part of your job and ask yourself whether you feel comfortable with it. If you work with antiques when basically material things don't interest you, you will feel uncomfortable. If you're more inclined to champion the underdog and your boss wants you to act otherwise, you won't be thrilled about work. If the pressure is on to make profits when you're more interested in quality, your personal belief system will be compromised.

When we're living and working authentically and following the path we know is right, motivation is less of a major problem although there will still be odd days when it all seems uphill. If you feel your battle is a major one, take some time to think about whether you need to make some fundamental adjustments to bring the sort of work you do more in line with your own personal beliefs.

Way 83 The future today

The future often causes us concern. Will this happen? Will that happen? What if nothing happens? We can worry enough to bring ourselves to a complete halt. Against a welter of anxieties our feeble motivation stands little chance of blossoming forth.

Yet no amount of worrying about things which might or might not happen ever changed a thing. Thinking about the future, one which doesn't yet exist apàrt from in our minds, achieves nothing. While we're doing that, we're doing nothing else – we're not getting on with our work. Leaving worries behind can be, well, worrying – at first. It might seem to us that if we do that, we won't be doing anything about whatever dread we might be anticipating. But bringing ourselves back into the here and now brings us to the point where we can actually start affecting what will happen. The future starts now.

Whatever we do, or don't do, is crucial. If you get down to writing the report it will affect your future in one way; if you don't, it will still affect it in another way. Inactivity may put things on hold but can lead to an unpleasant outcome. Instead, within each moment lies the opportunity to shape the sort of future we want for ourselves. We can, from this very moment, start to realise our dreams, ambitions – as well as our everyday targets.

Do what you need to do in order to start making a better future. Do it now. And if you think that by putting off your work you can opt out of the game plan, think again. Remember that what you *don't* do also affects things. So pick up the pen, plug in the computer and start changing your future *now*.

Way 84 Smile, please

Whatever goes on in the mind is reflected in the face. No news there. We know that when we feel worried, anxious or sad our faces register it. Frown lines, furrowed brows and down-turned mouths show to the world what's going on inside. No doubt if you're feeling miserable about work and utterly uninspired right now your face, and body, will hardly be hiding the fact.

What many people are not aware of is that the traffic flows both ways, so to speak. According to research smiling, even when when we don't feel happy, has a beneficial effect on our bodies. As Liz Hodgkinson says in her book *Smile Therapy*, '… if you force yourself to smile, or indeed to simulate any emotion by adopting the appropriate facial expression, that emotion will soon be felt in the brain and body'.

So if you're feeling down in the mouth, try turning it up at the corners to see what happens. Put a smile on your face and notice how it makes you feel. It doesn't matter if you have nothing to smile about; just do it. And do it regularly. The effects wear off after a while, so remember to beam again every now and then – especially when you have to tackle a new piece of work. And beam even more if it's something you really don't want to do.

Feeling motivated makes us feel good but, if smile therapy is anything to go by, instead of waiting for motivation to come *before* you can feel better, try smiling to encourage it along. You may not feel happy to start with, but keep smiling and you soon will.

Way 85 Frozen with fear

When children are reprimanded by unthinking parents and teachers for doing things incorrectly it makes them feel stupid, ashamed, and downright miserable. If it happens frequently enough, they automatically become hesitant about even trying the next time they have to attempt something new. If trying and failing usually turns out to be such an unpleasant experience for them, there's a certain wisdom in deciding it may be best to avoid trying at all.

Unfortunately, this learned behaviour can be carried into adulthood. When presented with a new or challenging situation or piece of work, without even thinking about it, we fall back into our old ways. Subconsciously we become a child again, fearing that if we make an attempt at what needs doing we'll incur the wrath of the Big People again. Not unnaturally, in this frame of mind, we may decide to give it all a miss. No thankyou. Not that again. Frozen with fear, we achieve nothing. I'll go and have a cup of coffee instead, we think, read the newspaper or potter about tidying up the desk; something which doesn't involve any risk of failure.

The situation calls for reassurance. First, acknowledge your fear of failure. Then start to get to grips with the fact that we all do it; we all fail at times; we all fall short of the mark despite our best efforts. It's part of the process – it's how we learn. Often it can be the best way to learn, and it's certainly what an expert in any field will have done many times on their way to the top.

If fear of failure is keeping you frozen to the spot, unable to get on with tackling what needs doing, remember it's OK to fail. What's not OK is to avoid trying.

Way 86 Long-term motivation

According to management guru Peter Drucker, using carrots and sticks to motivate staff simply doesn't work; not consistently and not for long periods, anyway. Rewards only lead to us wanting more and more – and more. In the work setting he believes more effective long-term motivation is achieved through '… embracing responsibility for the organization and its contribution to the larger society…'.

We have looked at our personal goals and followed our own wider life aims but, apparently, we also need to take into account the company we work for, its place in the community at large and the impact it may have on that community. And you thought you were just a marketing manager/secretary/personnel officer! Obviously there's more to feeling motivated than meets the eye.

Taking on board what Drucker suggests means we ought to give more than just a passing thought to the company we work for; not just what it produces or sells and not just what the boss is like. We need to look at the whole shooting match. We even need to look at what effect the business is having on society, both intentionally and unintentionally. If you find you deplore what your employer is doing you're hardly likely to be enthused about turning up for work every day to make your contribution. Basically, you won't feel motivated.

To make sure your long-term motivation is on firm ground, take a tip from Drucker and wholeheartedly embrace responsibility for your company and the contribution it's making. Go on. Give it a hug.

Way 87 Energy conservation

Children love new toys. So do adults – they just have bigger, more expensive ones. But no new toy can hold anyone's attention forever. The same goes for work. Our attention wanders; we lose interest; we get tired of doing the same thing hour after hour. Change is vitally important to refresh and maintain our interest – and our energy levels.

Some tasks have to be seen through in one go, but there may be others which can be tackled intermittently. The act of switching from one task to another stimulates interest again and gives a boost to energy reserves – without having to resort to caffeine or sugar.

Think about how you approach your work. Do you tend to think that, once started, you must see each task through to the end at a single sitting? Do you find yourself tiring half-way through your work? Do you keep getting bored? If you tend to try and hold on till the bitter end you may not be doing your motivation levels any favours. Try to make a point of breaking off from a task *before* you start getting tired. Put it to one side while you still feel good about doing it. In this way you'll have positive associations with the task when you pick it up again, perhaps later in the day or after you've spent half an hour on something completely different.

We may be creatures of habit, but change also plays its part in keeping us motivated. Introduce more of it into the way you work and you could find it goes some way to solving your motivation problems.

> 'Whenever I'm caught between two evils, I take the one I never tried.'
>
> *Mae West*

Way 88 Cramming

People have very different ways of working. Some like to work at a consistent pace; some like to get work out of the way as quickly as possible; and a great many of us seem to spend the greater part of the time thinking about deadlines but not actually doing anything until the very last moment. The intense pressure of having to complete work by a certain time or date is the only thing which motivates us sufficiently to do anything at all. Changing the habit is one option, or else we can, as interior designers would say, make a feature of it.

Accept that this is how you work, and perhaps even work best. But instead of letting all that time go by simply worrying about what you have to do and playing mental games with yourself about it, fill it with other work. That's right. Cram another piece of work in ahead of it. Arrange for a deadline to take you up to when you know you really will have to make a start on the other project. Start arranging deadlines crammed up close to each other.

If you're going to adopt this strategy, you also need to plan time for a work-free period to follow. If you're working under such pressure you're going to need it. But so that the time off doesn't turn into full, feature-length time out, plan to have a new workload which must be started immediately on your 'due back' date.

Pressure is something most of us try to avoid whenever we can, but if it really is the only way you seem able to get down to doing anything at all, then make it work for you instead.

Way 89 Are you well?

When you're glowing with health everything is much easier. You feel on top of things. You have the energy, stamina and vitality to cope with whatever the day demands. On the other hand, you know that if you're feeling unwell, perhaps coming down with a cold or coping with a hangover, no matter how much you may want to work, the body (including the brain) is unable to oblige.

If you're fully aware there's a good reason for feeling under par, that's fine. However, there may be times when, although not exactly feeling unwell, we know we can feel better.

When you're struggling with work and just don't seem to have the enthusiasm you normally have, it's worth checking out your health. Sometimes we just don't realise we're not up to scratch. So long as we can still walk to the coffee machine we assume we're fine. It's like a friend of mine who was recently finding things a struggle but kept on regardless. On eventually going to her doctor she discovered she was chronically anaemic and was put on a course of iron tablets straight away. Now she's her normal perky self, coping with an incredibly demanding lifestyle with consummate ease.

Without turning into a hypochondriac it's worth remembering to ask of ourselves what we ask others as a matter of course when they're finding things a struggle: 'Are you well?' If you're not, it may simply be a cold coming on, but what is for sure is that you can't expect to be highly motivated if you're not feeling in the peak of good health. If you have any health concerns, good GPs are always happy to check things out and offer reassurance where it's needed.

Way 90 In the mood?

Our emotions are powerful things; so powerful that they can affect how well our bodies work. Someone who is depressed may have lowered vitality; receiving good news can make us jump for joy. At work, if our emotions aren't in good shape we're unlikely to feel motivated to do much at all.

If there are good reasons for feeling low, make sure you are getting the support you need from friends and family to help you through. When it's more than just an upset, counselling is often helpful. Your GP should be able to advise, or you could arrange to see someone privately. If you have work-related worries, talk them through with your line manager or another person who can help.

Apart from life's ups and downs, our diet also has an important part to play in affecting how we feel. Eating poorly not only affects our bodies and the amount of energy we have at our disposal, it also affects our minds. For example, Vitamin B1 deficiency leads to problems with concentration, memory loss and confusion, among other things. Vitamin B12 deficiencies can cause similar problems. Insufficient potassium brings on irritability and mental disorientation. Amino acids also play an important part in regulating our mental states and the functions of the brain.

If your moods cause you problems for no real reason, check out your diet. Make sure you're eating in a healthy, well-balanced way. If you're in any doubt a good multi-vitamin and mineral supplement may help, but do check things out with your GP. Feeling good about work may depend on improving how you feel in yourself.

Working places

The workplace environment has a bearing on how we feel about pitching up every day and settling down to do our job. Of course, if we loathe what we do no amount of plush office space will make us want to do it more, but trying to carry out our duties in an unsuitable environment can take its toll on our motivation. I once had to spend part of my working week in a narrow, dingy, windowless room. Needless to say, on those days work was always a struggle, despite the fact that I enjoyed the job itself.

At the extreme end of the scale, a place of work can be so unsuitable as to pose health and safety hazards. Rickety chairs, inadequate heating and ventilation and poor storage facilities may be tolerated by staff; but bad seating can lead to back and other muscle strain problems, poor heating and ventilation can be in direct contravention of health and safety regulations, and unstable piles of boxes or other items are accidents waiting to happen. Hopefully, most of us don't have to put up with such conditions but even so, familiarity makes it is easy to overlook the fact that our workplace may not be helping us work as effectively as we might.

Our motivation needs stimulation to keep it alive. Improving the work environment won't change the work itself but it can improve how we feel about sitting down to get on with it in the first place. You don't have to be an interior designer and nor does a major refurbishment have to take place. Much can be done to improve what is already there.

The following ten Ways concentrate on ideas for making where you work a place where your motivation can happily survive, and perhaps even thrive.

Way 91 Green it up

Plants are a relatively cheap, simple way to improve a room instantly. If you don't believe the impact they can make, take a look at a few interior design magazines and imagine the rooms shown *without* the plants.

You may have your own favourites, but 'architectural' plants tend to work better than a mass of weeny pots, which can make a place look worse. According to the size of the room, work out how many plants you need or, if you're taking unilateral action, simply decide on which plant would work best in the area or space available to you.

Pay some attention to location. A bright, sunny position will suit different plants from those happiest in a north-facing room. Also think about radiators and temperature ranges throughout the day, and night. If you're not sure, ask for advice from garden centre or florist's staff. Also think about where to place plants so they don't become a hindrance.

Apart from cheering a place up, remember greenery also helps, in its own small way, to improve the air quality by providing a useful oxygen boost.

Way 92 Cheer it up

A quick lick of paint on the walls of an office can do wonders to brighten up the whole feel of a place. If your workplace looks grimmer than Steptoe's back room there's probably room for improvement.

Deciding whether to redecorate is obviously easier for those running their own business. For employees it may be a simple case of bringing it to the boss's attention and, perhaps, offering to help out with the decorating, if appropriate. If you're working in a large office it may be a little more difficult; cost-cutting measures being what they are, decorating the workplace for employees may not be seen as a priority. It may come down to putting a convincing enough argument forward about improving staff morale and productivity. Put it in words which they will understand and again, if it's appropriate, make an offer to help out with the work.

Way 93 Shelves

Anyone who has moved into their first unfurnished place and tried to live without a chest of drawers knows how desperate life can get. I thought I would be able to cope for a time but soon realised the drawbacks of not being able to stay organised and quickly find what was needed.

In the office, the same applies. It is vitally important to have enough suitable shelf and storage space in order to organise your work and have an environment which isn't cluttered up with piles and piles of disorganised mess on floors, desk tops, spare chairs and any other available surface. Otherwise, work becomes a chore and, ultimately, demotivating when the whole room has to be turned upside down just to find the information you need.

Make sure you have sufficient storage spaces and that they are serving you well. If necessary, invest in more shelves, filing cabinets or other storage systems. It can help to make each small task take less of a Herculean effort to complete.

Way 94 Clear the way

Despite taking affirmative action with paperwork and files, there may still come a time when room space starts to take on a distinctly pint pot quality. Instead of trying to work around the difficulties and frustrations created by full filing cabinets, crammed cupboards and stuffed shelves, there's a simple way in which to generate more space: box up redundant material and put it into storage.

Without a regular weeding out process it is easy for old files to accumulate almost unnoticed, taking up valuable space which is needed for current projects. Sort through the paperwork which, though necessary to keep, is no longer active. Place it in archive boxes, marked up, and store away elsewhere. Large amounts can be put into secure paid storage facilities; otherwise, use available cupboard space or other nooks and crannies which are safe, secure and where the material can easily be accessed when needed – you don't want to create more problems for yourself later on when an old file needs to be resurrected.

Clearing away old material can be another way not only to make more breathing space, but also to make your working life simpler.

Way 95 Blinds

Office windows tend not to receive quite as much attention

as perhaps they ought. It is not unusual, especially in smaller enterprises, to leave them undressed and, while curtain ruffles aren't appropriate, having nothing at all can create problems – especially in summer.

Direct sunlight streaming into a room can produce an almost instant hot-house effect which, when combined with the heat generated by office equipment and human bodies, can make for an uncomfortable environment. Sunshine can also cause problems with glare – off computer screens and paperwork. Besides creating eye-strain, this increases the likelihood of unnecessary mistakes being made – a frustrating and demotivating experience in itself.

Think about whether you would feel more comfortable, and your work be enhanced, by solving the problems created by direct sunlight. Blinds are often the best solution – either vertical, horizontal or roller. See which ones would work best in your place of work.

Way 96 Pictures

Every time I look up from my work I see one of my favourite prints, a bright abstract splash of blue, white and yellow reminding me of long days spent by the Mediterranean. I always feel better, uplifted, after a quick glance in its direction. I wouldn't be without it, and in its own small way it plays a part in helping me through the working day.

Take a quick look at the pictures which surround you. If they are non-existent, or so dingy no one can make them out any more, it may be time for a change. Introducing new wall hangings may be outside the realms of possibility in your workplace, in which case think about using smaller copies of prints you find inspiring: a stand-up frame on your desktop, a print on the cover of your desk diary, a postcard within easy reach when you need it.

If you would like a little inspiration when you look up from the gloomy depths of the work in front of you, think about how you might bring some artwork into your working life.

Way 97 Pinboards

Many offices have them, but all too often they are cluttered with redundant notices and forgotten fliers. Yet pinboards can be useful devices, and not just for carrying missives from the management.

Pinboards can be used to create a space which plays its part in helping to motivate by attaching items such as inspiring or humorous quotations, affirmations, and favourite images. Make it a dynamic space; keep its displays constantly changing so there's always something new to stimulate you when you glance in its direction. Reminders of personal aims, daily targets, mission statements, even bank statements can all be included – whatever you find motivating at any given time.

We need external stimulation to inject a fresh note of optimism when our enthusiasm starts to sag throughout the day. A pinboard can be a useful tool for carrying those messages we find supportive, uplifting – and, hopefully, motivational.

Way 98 Flowers

Flowers are another simple way in which to humanise and naturalise the working environment, and to make us feel better about settling down to a day's work which we may not exactly be feeling inspired to do. Having a fresh, ever-changing vase of bright blooms rings the changes – change which provides the stimulation we need on a regular basis. More 'alternative' types might say it's also a symbolic way in which to keep us connected with the earth (they could be right).

Displays needn't be flamboyant or expensive. Raid the petty cash and buy whatever flowers are in season, or bring in contributions from the garden. A small bunch displayed well in an attractive vase, or even a single flower, does just as well as more exotic arrangements. The important thing is to be able to feast your eyes on a display of nature's best.

Way 99 Feng Shui

This ancient Chinese mystical art is gaining popularity in the West – even big businesses use it. It is a way of ensuring that the chi, or energy, in houses and offices flows in a beneficial and harmonious way. When it flows well it is said to bring happiness, peace, prosperity and good luck; when it doesn't, you may be in for a rocky ride.

According to feng shui principles, the way energy flows is affected by the location of doors, furniture, mirrors and water, as well as things like the shape and function of a room. Feng shui practitioners assess a property and suggest ways in which to remedy any faults to beneficial effect. If money disappears as fast as it comes in it could be your front door's fault; if relationships are problematic your bed may be facing the wrong way.

Feng shui reminds us of our connection with our environment. If you feel yours could be hindering your progress at work rather than helping, feng shui might have some interesting solutions. Heard of sick building syndrome? This could be the answer.

Way 100 Ionisers

More workplaces are now becoming non-smoking environments – a blessed relief to all those who don't smoke. Trying to work in a smelly, smoke-filled room when you're not a smoker yourself is not the most conducive environment for trying to plug in the concentration and turn it full on. Better for all is the sort of atmosphere you're more likely to find at the seaside or in the fresh open countryside – but unfortunately sitting at your desk on the beach isn't an option for most of us.

One way in which to bring that freshness into the office is by using an ioniser. These dinky machines generate a constant flow of negatively charged ions which attract fine particles of pollutants thereby neutralising them. Instead of floating around in the air waiting for us to breathe them in they become grounded to nearby surfaces or, if the ioniser has a filter attachment, they can be extracted. They also help counter the negative effect of office equipment.

The manufacturers of these machines claim a variety of benefits, from promoting a sense of well-being right through to helping to alleviate depression. At the very least ionisers are a cheap, effective way of making sure the air in which you work feels cleaner and less polluted, and may be just what you need to help you think more clearly and stay refreshed right through the working day.

Way 101 It's a dream

We are all individuals, and no one solution to the problem of self-motivation will suit everybody; what inspires one person will leave another cold, and vice versa. And being the complex creatures we are, what unblocks the log jam one day won't do a thing for us the next: sometimes we need only a gentle push to get us going; at others, a stick of dynamite.

Motivation seems to have something of a fickle, and often obstinate, nature. It can be put off by the smallest thing – but then encouraged just as easily. The challenge for each of us is to start understanding its many quirks, preferences and dislikes in each of the myriad situations it is likely to find itself throughout each working day.

As you start to understand a little more about how your own motivation responds best under different circumstances and to different challenges, you may come across other strategies which work well. They may be adaptations of suggestions you've read here, or they may be new ideas which emerge out of trial and error. What you may also find is that a mix-and-match approach works best. Some suggestions could become permanent features – new ways of working, changes to the workplace – and serve to underpin other strategies which are used singly, collaboratively or sequentially. Eventually a blueprint could emerge which serves you well in the majority of instances when motivation has gone walkabout.

Be persistent. Experiment. Try different approaches. And hopefully you'll eventually find the ones which work best for you.

Bibliography

Drucker, Peter (1997) *Management: Tasks, Responsibilities, Practices*, Butterworth Heinemann, UK.

Hodgkinson, Liz (1987) *Smile Therapy*, Optima, UK.

Austin, Valerie (1994) *Self Hypnosis*, Thorsons, UK.

Robbins, Anthony (1988) *Unlimited Power*, Simon & Schuster, UK.

McGregor, Douglas (1985) *The Human Side of Enterprise* (Second Edition), Penguin, UK.

Herzberg, Frederick (1993) *The Motivation to Work*, Transaction Publishers, USA.

Maslow, Abraham (1943) *A Theory of Human Motivation*, Psychological Review, vol 50, pp370–96.

Mervyn, Leonard (1994) *Thorsons Complete Guide to Vitamins and Minerals*, Earl Mindell Arlington Books UK.